focus on the family®
women's series

W9-AWU-804

WOMEN OF
Worth

Gospel Light

PUBLISHED BY GOSPEL LIGHT
VENTURA, CALIFORNIA, U.S.A.
Gospel Light PRINTED IN THE U.S.A.

Gospel Light is a Christian publisher dedicated to serving the local church. We believe God's vision for Gospel Light is to provide church leaders with biblical, user-friendly materials that will help them evangelize, disciple and minister to children, youth and families.

It is our prayer that this Gospel Light resource will help you discover biblical truth for your own life and help you minister to others. May God richly bless you.

For a free catalog of resources from Gospel Light, please call your Christian supplier or contact us at 1-800-4-GOSPEL *or* www.gospellight.com.

PUBLISHING STAFF
William T. Greig, Chairman · **Dr. Elmer L. Towns,** Senior Consulting Publisher · **Natalie Clark,** Product Line Manager · **Pam Weston,** Managing Editor · **Jessie Minassian,** Editorial Assistant **Bayard Taylor, M.Div.,** Senior Editor, Biblical and Theological Issues · **Rosanne Moreland,** Cover and Internal Designer · **Flora Washburn,** Contributing Writer

ISBN 0-8307-3336-1
© 2004 Focus on the Family
All rights reserved.
Printed in the U.S.A.

Any omission of credits is unintentional. The publisher requests documentation for future printings.

WOMEN OF WORTH

Who am I? Why do I have so much and yet feel such discontent? What keeps me from truly being the person I want to be? How can I grow deeper in my relationships? Why am I so fat? Why am I so skinny? Ugh, I have a gray hair! Why am I always the serious one? Will I ever grow up? Why, oh why, oh why?—the thoughts go on, don't they?

We all have thoughts that challenge our feelings of self-worth and our identity. We are either striving to be like another person or struggling *not* to be like someone else. Some of us want to climb the tallest mountain; others are content to stay at home. Some seem to have fabulous lives; others are wrenched by neglect or abuse. From various walks of life we come: young and old, single and married, career oriented and staying at home, wealthy and eking out a living. We all look in the mirror and ask, *Who am I?*

Women often define themselves based on what is expected of them. They are bound by perceived expectations placed on them by parents, other family members and friends; by pressures of the world—work, society, children, marriage, sexuality, relationships and so much more—and by their personal perceptions and expectations. Misperceptions or wrong expectations say that we don't measure up, that we are not good enough, or that we need to do more or try harder. This study will help you see who you are—not as the world sees you but as God sees you—helping you appreciate your uniqueness and grow in your relationships with Christ Jesus and with others.

This study is a holistic approach, dealing with your whole being: body, soul, mind and spirit. It is hard to live out God's love for you until you appreciate who you are as a whole person, including the physical, spiritual, mental and emotional abilities, limitations and circumstances that God has given you. These lessons have been chosen based on a natural progression of issues with which women deal. They are not exhaustive but are meant to bring clarity to—and an appreciation for—who you are. By tackling relevant issues that you face every day, your relationship with God will be rejuvenated, you will realize that you don't have to be a superwoman to feel valued, and you will be able to say "I like being a woman and desire to be the woman God intends me to be."

FOCUS ON THE FAMILY'S WOMEN'S MINISTRY SERIES

And this is my prayer: that your love may abound more and more in knowledge and depth of insight, so that you may be able to discern what is best and may be pure and blameless until the day of Christ, filled with the fruit of righteousness that comes through Jesus Christ—to the glory and praise of God.

PHILIPPIANS 1:9-11

The goal of this series is to help women identify who they are, based on their unique nature and in the light of God's Word. We hope that each woman who is touched by this series will understand her heavenly Father's unfathomable love for her and that her life has a divine purpose and value. This series also has a secondary goal: That as women pursue their relationship with God, they will also understand the importance of building relationships with other women to enrich their own lives and grow personally, as well as help others understand their God-given worth and purpose.

Session Overview

Women of Worth can be used in a variety of situations, including small-group Bible studies, Sunday School classes or mentoring relationships. An individual can also use this book as an at-home study tool.

Each session contains four main components.

Everyday Woman

This section introduces the topic for the session by giving you a personal glimpse into the life of an ordinary woman—someone you can relate to—and it asks probing questions to help you focus on the theme of the session.

Eternal Wisdom

This is the Bible study portion in which you will read Scripture and answer questions to help discover lasting truths from God's Word.

Enduring Hope

This section provides questions and commentary that encourage you to place your hope in God's plan.

Everyday Life

A time to reflect on ways that the Lord is calling you to change, suggesting steps you can take to get there. It is also a time for the whole group to pray and encourage one another.

Journaling

We encourage you to keep a journal while you are working through this study. A personal journal chronicles your spiritual journey, recording prayers, thoughts and events along the way. Reviewing past journal entries is a faith-building exercise that allows you to see how God has worked in your life—by resolving a situation, changing an attitude, answering your prayers or helping you grow more like Christ.

Leader's Discussion Guide

A leader's discussion guide is included at the end of this book to help leaders encourage participation, lead discussions and develop relationships.

There are additional helps for leading small groups or mentoring relationships in *The Focus on the Family Women's Ministry Guide*.

DEFINING
Worth

For you created my inmost being; you knit me together in my
mother's womb. I praise you because I am fearfully and wonderfully made;
your works are wonderful, I know that full well.

PSALM 139:13-14

EVERYDAY WOMAN

It was a warm autumn day. Jamie sat on a park bench, contemplating her life and wondering how she had gotten to where she now was. She grew up in an average family, but there was never an expression of love or acceptance. All she heard from her parents was "Do it better," "Do it this way," and "Why can't you get it the first time?" She had a few friends, but she never felt accepted. Her mind raced through different events and situations. She still remembered comments that were made to her and how they affected her at the time. Finally, she challenged a statement that a coworker, Karen, had told her: that God loved her.

How can He? Why should He? Jamie had wondered.

A smile began to form on Jamie's face, remembering how Karen had lovingly and patiently helped her understand so much about herself. Now she was beginning to understand how God's love for her could reshape her life into one of value and self-worth. She reached for the Bible sitting next to her, turned to her favorite passage—Psalm 139—and began to read about the depth of His commitment to her. Jamie was beginning to understand her own value to God. It had been hard for her to believe that anyone really loved and accepted her as she was, let alone God. After many years of struggling with who she was and what value she had, she was finally beginning to believe that God did love her after all. With the help of a friend, she was beginning to understand that real self-worth was based on who she was created to be and on her relationship with God.[1]

⚘

Psalm 139 is a beautiful picture of God's great care in creating each one of us. Take a few moments to read this psalm.

A woman's feelings of value and self-worth are wrapped up in her past and present experiences. All the facets of her life influence her perception of who she is as a person. From the moment she is conceived, there are thoughts and experiences that lead to how she identifies herself as a person. There are positive and negative events that take place in the home, on the playground, in school, at church, in the media, in relationships, in marriage, in divorce, in dysfunctional relationships, during the death of a loved one—the list goes on. Each woman can relate to events or experiences in her life that have created negative and positive feelings of personal worth. These events shape us, but our challenge is to separate the experiences in our lives from our true identity, based on our relationship with a loving, forgiving God. Answer the following questions with that in mind.

1. List five words to describe yourself besides being God's daughter.

2. Write a short statement that explains who you are as a woman.

3. How would you define "self-worth"?

4. Is there a difference between self-worth and self-esteem? Explain.

It is important to note that positive, or healthy, self-worth is not related to exalting ourselves or thinking more highly of ourselves than we should. This has been a misconception in some Christian circles. A healthy self-worth actually strengthens our Christian walk, helping us to walk in humility as we love God and love one another.

ETERNAL WISDOM

Our hope lies not in who we are but in who God is. He has created us in His image (see Genesis 1:27), yet we so often forget this fact and live our lives far short of what God has called us to be. Psalm 139 is a beautiful depiction of God's greatness and His love for us, His creation. It not only gives us hope but also the reassurance that God does know us. In fact, He knows us much better than we know ourselves.

5. Psalm 139:13-14 captures the heart of the chapter. Write a sentence to describe what each of the following phrases mean:

"For you created my inmost being;"

"You knit me together in my mother's womb."

"I am fearfully and wonderfully made;"

"Your works are wonderful, I know that full well."

6. Summarize what these verses say about you.

7. Do you agree with what you have just written? Explain.

There is more to examine in Psalm 139 that offers an understanding of God's attitude toward us. We not only see Him as creator, but we also see other attributes that affirm His love.

8. Reread Psalm 139, underlining or noting the words and phrases that stand out to you. (You may write them in your journal or on a sheet of paper.)

ENDURING HOPE

There are many situations that keep us from believing that God loves us and has a unique purpose for each of us. In the opening story, Jamie's environment coupled with her own perceptions negatively influenced her feelings of self-worth, making her feel unloved and unaccepted. As she grew up, her sense of self-worth became dependent on how productive she was and whether she did a good enough job. Before she began to understand what Karen was telling her about God's love, there were days when she felt she would never amount to anything.

9. List circumstances, people and events that have had a negative impact on your life.

    Put a check mark by those that are unresolved.

    How have those things you listed affected who you are and how you live your life?

10. How does Psalm 56:3-4 relate to circumstances or people that have a negative effect on you?

11. Rewrite Psalm 51:10-12 as a prayer.

There may be a situation or person in your life that you feel you will never be able to forgive. What is important is how you allow issues to continue to affect you. Are you ready to let the Lord peel the layers of hurt and painful experiences from you so that He can restore you to your God-given identity? It may take time, but God is faithful.[2]

Understanding our self-worth is the beginning of the process. The next step is to change how we think about ourselves. If we believe what is written in the Scriptures about God and His love for us, then we can begin to reclaim the positive thoughts that He says about us and toward us. Instead of saying "I will never amount to anything," we can begin to say "I am God's daughter; He made me and He loves me. Furthermore, He has a plan for my life, and He will help me understand it."

12. Looking back on this session, what area would you like to bring before the Lord for healing?

There is one part of Psalm 139:14 that we didn't cover previously: "I praise you because . . ." Praising God is the first step in discovering our value to Him. It is an acknowledgment that God is good, that He loves us and that we love Him.

13. Begin by praising God for who He is. Read the following verses and then make a list of the reasons you have to praise the Lord. Use your journal if you need more room.

   - "Praise him for his acts of power; praise him for his surpassing greatness" (Psalm 150:2).
   - "Let everything that has breath praise the LORD" (Psalm 150:6).
   - "I will praise the LORD all my life; I will sing praise to my God as long as I live" (Psalm 146:2).
   - "Great is our Lord and mighty in power; his understanding has no limit" (Psalm 147:5).

Continue to add to this list throughout this study. Whenever you are having a difficult day, refer to this list to jump-start your praise.

14. Jamie has begun her journey of rediscovering God's design in her life. Her understanding of Psalm 139 has been instrumental in her holding on to God's love when the haunting memories of rejection begin to play in her head. In question 5 you were asked to read Psalm 139. In question 8 you were asked to underline or note words and phrases that stood out to you. Now pull these together to form your own paraphrase of Psalm 139. Write this as a letter to God in the space below.

God is a God of creativity! If there is another artistic format (drawing, painting, singing, sculpting, dancing, etc.) that would help you express what is in your heart, use that instead.

It is okay to say that you are having difficulty believing that God loves you or that you are "fearfully and wonderfully made," if that is how you feel. The important thing is to be able to recognize and express God's love for you, and then to learn to praise Him for who you are, even in your imperfect state. God is greater than your weaknesses and hurts. Ask Him to transform you by renewing your mind and strengthening your heart (see Romans 12:2).

In the next seven sessions we will explore different facets of womanhood. May God bless you as you travel this journey of self-discovery and as you learn what it means to be a woman worthy of God's love.

Notes

1. This is a fictional account. Any resemblance to actual events or people, living or dead, is purely coincidental.
2. Certain issues may require professional help. You can seek help from your pastor or ask for a referral to a professional Christian counselor.

Who AM I?

Your hands made me and formed me;
give me understanding to learn your commands.

PSALM 119:73

❧

EVERYDAY WOMAN

It was Sarah's birthday. She was a sweet, soft-spoken lady whom everyone liked. She was always willing to help if asked, and she never disagreed with the group's decision regarding what the next project should be. Decision making was not something Sarah liked to do.

Jane was excited. They were having a surprise party for Sarah at Jane's house, and she wanted it to be festive and fun. She spent hours looking for the right decorations and planning the party. On her way home she realized that she had forgotten to pick up the cake. She frantically drove back to the store, making it home in time to see Monica standing on her doorstep.

Monica was waiting anxiously. She had arrived 15 minutes early to make sure everything was perfect for the party and was disturbed that Jane wasn't even home. When Christy pulled into Jane's driveway, she began pulling bags out of her car and giving assignments to everyone who was there to help. Jane made a joke about being late; then she began pulling the decorations out of the bags and piling them on the table. Monica sighed and began to move the decorations to a side table so that she could set the table properly.

Each glass, fork, spoon, knife and plate had to be placed just so.

Christy began to complain that they were taking too much time. She wanted them to just get the work done and quit being so picky. Monica felt insulted by Christy's need to control, but she kept her feelings to herself. Jane just laughed, brushed off Christy's comments and kept working.

Finally, it was time for the party. The guests began arriving and prepared for Sarah's entrance. Soon Sarah walked in, thinking she was there to pick up Jane for lunch. "Surprise!" everyone shouted. Sarah looked around, taking it all in but keeping her excitement on the inside. She smiled and gave Jane a hug.

The party was a success. Jane was thrilled. Christy knew they could not have done it without her organization. Monica wished she could have done a better job. Sarah felt loved and appreciated. At the end the four friends hugged one another and laughed about their time together.[1]

⚭

Women are great! We are all gifted with unique temperaments (personalities) that define our talents, abilities and emotions. The purpose of this session is to help us recognize the personality God designed in us so that we can know ourselves better, appreciate our strengths and improve on our weaknesses. It is an opportunity to understand why we act and react the way we do. It will also help us understand why others act as they do.

One way of looking at personality is the fourfold basic temperaments model.[2] According to this model, we are each a blend of four basic temperaments with one type generally standing out more than the rest. Our goal here is to recognize these basic temperaments and see which one (or which combination) best describes who we are. This is an invaluable tool because it helps us understand ourselves (and others) better and realize that we really are okay. God may have made you with strong leadership abilities or with a servant's heart. He may have created you with a joyful spirit or with a desire to bring peace to the world. Understanding how God has uniquely created each of us helps us grow in appreciation of our value to God and to our world. Rather than trying to bury our personalities, we need to understand them so that, with great relief, we can say, "That's why I act the way I do!" Understanding our temperaments begins with knowing that God has created each of us with His purpose and plan in mind (see Ephesians 2:10).

Let's have a look at one simple, fourfold temperament model for understanding personality.[3] These temperaments are divided into two groups: extroverts and introverts. Extroverts are outgoing and outwardly expressive, preferring to be around people. In this model, extroverted personalities include sanguines and cholerics. Introverts are more reflective and contemplative, preferring moments of solitude. Introvert personalities are melancholics and phlegmatics. Let's discover more about these four personality types.

Sanguines love to have fun. Put them in a room with people, and they have a great time. They are easy to get along with; people generally like them. Sanguines are very expressive, enthusiastic and emotional; and they have a sense of humor, are creative and enjoy people. They need attention, affection, approval and acceptance. On the downside, they are usually considered scatterbrained or disorganized, not detail oriented, often gullible or naïve, and seldom serious minded.

1.   Who do you know that is a sanguine? Describe that person's predominant traits.

Cholerics are considered natural-born leaders. They are the ones who get things done—their way. Cholerics believe they are always right and know exactly the way something should be handled. They are great in an emergency because they make quick, correct judgments, but they can sometimes blow the wind out of an unsuspecting sanguine who is not as organized or as driven. From others, cholerics need to feel a sense of obedience, appreciation for accomplishments and credit for a job well done. In the negative, cholerics are often considered too bossy, insensitive or impatient.

2.   Who do you know who exhibits the leadership qualities of a choleric? List his or her qualities.

Melancholics are thinkers. Many artists, poets and musicians are melancholics. Their analytical minds also make them great in mathematic and engineering fields. Much more reserved than extroverts, melancholics prefer a quiet atmosphere and choose friends cautiously. They often exhibit a servant's heart from which other temperaments can learn. They have a need for a sense of stability, space, silence and support. On the downside, melancholics can become moody and easily depressed. Perfectionist attitudes can also give way to criticism of self and others.

3. Do you know someone who has melancholic tendencies? Explain your choice.

Phlegmatics are natural peacemakers. They are the quiet observers in the group, content to sit back and take one day at a time without getting their feathers ruffled. Phlegmatics get along with practically everybody. They need a sense of respect, feeling of worth and emotional support. Being easygoing and content are great qualities, but when taken to the extreme, the phlegmatic can be seen as indecisive, lazy and unmotivated. And under all that reserve, there is a hidden stubbornness.

4. Who is an easygoing peacemaker in your life? What other phlegmatic characteristics does this person have?

In our story, Jane was just interested in having a party—remembering all of the details was not a priority. Monica came early to make sure that everything would be done perfectly. Christy showed up ready for action, taking charge and pulling everything together. Sarah was the gentle, unemotional friend they all loved. The varying personality types of these four friends served to unite them in a paradoxical way.

5. Draw a line to the temperament that best describes each woman in our story.

Jane   Phlegmatic

Sarah   Choleric

Christy   Sanguine

Monica   Melancholic

Each of us might be a blend of two or more of these four personality types, but there is usually one dominant temperament that drives us.

6. Which of these personality traits best represents your temperament? Explain.

7. How can understanding your temperament help you appreciate your value?

8. How can understanding different temperaments help you appreciate the uniqueness of others?

9. What does Genesis 1:31 say about God's creation of you?

Discussing personality types doesn't mean that we put people—including ourselves—in little boxes with neatly tied bows around them. It is simply a tool to help us understand ourselves and to learn to appreciate others.

ETERNAL WISDOM

In Psalm 119:73, the writer acknowledged God as his creator. God formed every part—physical, emotional, spiritual and mental. Knowing this, the psalmist asked for understanding to know God's ways. As God forms people, He bestows different abilities and gifts based on His purposes for each person. Each of us has a particular contribution to give based on who we are.

Ephesians 2:10 says, "We are God's workmanship, created in Christ Jesus to do good works."

10. Look up the word "workmanship" in a dictionary. How does the dictionary's definition help you clarify the purpose for which you were created?

How should this verse affect the way we think about ourselves?

11. How has "being created anew in Christ Jesus" affected both your purpose in life and the expression of your innate personality characteristics?

Amazingly, when we begin to accept ourselves, we can begin to accept others and understand their strengths and weaknesses as well. We can tolerate—even appreciate—why someone else acts the way he or she does. While one person may love to be around a fun-loving person, someone else may consider this person irresponsible and loud. Someone may see a deep thinker as too serious. The strong leader in your life who gives great direction might be seen as bossy and controlling by another.

12. How does Matthew 7:1-5 relate to how we should react to others' personalities?

ENDURING HOPE

God has given each of us the ability to do certain things well (see Romans 12:6-8), but there are some strengths or abilities that need to be nurtured.

13. What personality strengths enable you to do something well?

14. List aspects of your personality that you have been trying to hide, whether out of fear of becoming prideful or because you just didn't understand that God created them for good.

15. What steps can you take to develop your strengths?

Ask God to show you a weakness that you could begin improving on. Don't focus on what others have said about you. Focus on what you hear God telling you in your heart. You might be surprised by what He has to say.

EVERYDAY LIFE

We have spent some time looking at basic temperament types using one model. Though we have not exhausted the subject, our goal has been to recognize that what God has created in you is good. Understanding and appreciating your temperament are vital parts of developing a healthy self-worth. The most important step you can take is to start believing what His Word has to say about you.

Growing in an understanding of your temperament involves exercising the gifts that God has given you to serve Christ's Body. First Peter 4:10 says, "Each one should use whatever gift he has received to serve others."

16. What gifts and skills has God given you?

How can you use them to serve others?

This week, focus on discovering how God can use you to serve the Body of Christ and your community. As you allow God to develop your strengths, ask Him to show you the best way you can love and serve others.

Take a moment to visualize your life as a masterpiece God is creating. See it as a work in progress. Thank Him for the strong qualities that you possess, and praise Him for perfecting the weak areas. Write a note to God expressing what you see, or draw a picture that expresses the masterpiece you see—in your journal or in the following space.

Notes

1. This is a fictional account. Any resemblance to actual events or people, living or dead, is purely coincidental.

2. This lesson is only an introduction to temperaments and is by no means exhaustive. There are many personality paradigms, and the purpose of using this fourfold model is simply to help you understand the basic strengths and weaknesses of different types of personality. For resources on other temperament models, visit Focus on the Family's website, www.family.org, and search "personality types."

3. Florence Littauer, *Personality Plus* (Tarrytown, NY: F. H. Revell, 1992).

IT'S MY *Body*

"Hear, O Israel, the Lord our God, the Lord is one. Love the Lord your God with all your heart and with all your soul and with all your mind and with all your strength." The second is this: "Love your neighbor as yourself."

MARK 12:29-31

EVERYDAY WOMAN

Millie, a lady in her 70s, was diagnosed with stage-four cancer. She was devastated. There were still so many things she wanted to do, like spend more time with her family and friends. Being a very active woman, it was hard for Millie to deal with what was happening. *Why, God?* her heart cried out.

Her family and friends by her side, she underwent major surgery to remove as much of the cancer as possible. Her doctor was optimistic that if she survived the surgery, she would survive the chemo treatments and have another year or so to enjoy. The surgery went very well. She was able to return home. A visiting nurse came in to help Millie's family care for her. During one of her visits, Carla, the nurse, asked Millie how she felt about everything that had happened. "Well, I must admit, I was in shock when I first heard about the cancer. I couldn't believe it was happening. I started to feel sorry for myself. Then one day I realized that God knows exactly what is going on. I want to live, but if He says it is time for me to go, I can't argue. I have to trust Him with my life and my family." Carla smiled at this woman whose strength and faith amazed her.

Eventually, Millie began to exercise. She noticed that her stamina picked up, and she didn't feel as depressed as she did when she just sat around the house. After the second chemo session, her hair began to fall out. She would look in the mirror and cry. Her daughter brought her scarves to wear and a hat to keep her head warm. Again, Millie decided to keep going. She felt better when she simply accepted what was not in her control.

People noticed that she seemed to get more beautiful. She began to shine from the inside out. "Millie, how do you do it?" her friend Jo asked.

"Well," Millie said, "I have great friends and family who are supporting me and loving me through all of this. God has been with me, and I know that my life is in His hands. Since I have been given a second chance, I am just not going to worry about the things that don't matter. My hair will grow back. Besides, I want to see what it looks like gray," Millie joked.

Jo looked at her with growing admiration because of the faith and hope she displayed. Jo didn't see an aged woman without hair; she saw a beautiful woman glowing with life![1]

⇛

The measure of a woman's value does not depend on how much she has accomplished in life, how much she weighs, what she looks like or even what others perceive to be her level of spirituality. A woman's self-worth is based on her ability to look in the mirror and like the woman she sees there. Determining self-worth is discovering the value of whom God created you to be. It is to acknowledge that your worth is based on God's love, grace and perfect design.

A major aspect of self-worth is to understand the importance of caring for the whole person: body, soul, mind and spirit. These areas are interrelated. Millie chose to let the spiritual, emotional and mental areas of her life override the reality of the physical. In so doing, she has led a fairly normal life in the midst of overwhelming circumstances.

1. In what ways did Millie show balance spiritually, physically, mentally and emotionally?

What would the quality of her life have been like if she had given in to the physical and the emotional, ignoring the other areas of her life?

It is important to look at the whole of who we are. The purpose of this session isn't to focus on whether you are fat or thin; it isn't about how smart or outwardly spiritual you are; it isn't about being happy all the time. This session is about caring for your whole self, focusing on how each area of your being affects the others and how the Lord can help you develop a balanced mind-set.

Mark 12:28-31 describes body, soul, mind and spirit.

Body—The Physical Me

Most of us think it would be great to be thin; others want to be taller or shorter. We play the comparison game: "If I just looked like . . . then my life would be perfect." Athletes are encouraged to work out hard and not gain a pound. Models starve themselves to keep their weight down, afraid they'll lose their appeal by the time they turn 30. Actresses find that the older they become, the harder it is to get leading-lady roles.

2. What happens to a woman who strives to perfect her body to gain the approval of others?

Should we give up on the idea of dieting? Yes, but only if we replace it with a desire to have a healthy body through good nutrition and exercise. "Exercise" can be a much-dreaded word. "I'm allergic to exercise," many would say. In our story, Millie learned that it helped her feel better. Just a few minutes a day lifted her spirits and increased her stamina.

3. What is the condition of your physical health? What would you desire it to be like 10, 20 or 30 years from now?

4. What impact does poor physical care have on your body? How does it affect your mind, emotions and walk with God?

Each of us is a spiritual being housed in a physical body. This shell may be temporal, but how we care for it will largely determine our quality and length of life.

Soul—The Emotional Me

Women are emotional creatures. Have you ever looked in the mirror and thought you couldn't look any better, only to be convinced the very next day that God could not have created a more hideous person? What caused such a shift in thinking from one day to the next? Several factors may have contributed. Maybe you ate a piece of chocolate cake and felt disgusted with yourself. Maybe you were premenstrual, or maybe someone said something that you took the wrong way. Perhaps you simply weren't feeling well. The cause doesn't matter; the point is that what you felt was very real that day. Positive and negative emotions can have lasting effects on us mentally, spiritually and physically.

5. How do negative emotions damage our well-being?

6. According to Proverbs 15:13, "A happy heart makes the face cheerful, but heartache crushes the spirit." How have you experienced this truth?

Our emotions are most closely tied to our thoughts.

Mind—The Thinking Me

The words that come from our mouths are the result of our thought processes, but the tone of our thoughts also affects our spiritual, emotional and physical well-being. Consider how another person's negative thoughts have affected you in the past, or how someone who always seems to look on the sunny side of things helps others feel better.

7. How does David's advice to his son, Solomon, in 1 Chronicles 28:9 relate to mental health?

Just as physical exercise is important for a healthy body, the mind also needs to be exercised. A healthy mind yields a healthier you.

Spiritual—The Lord in Me

Our spiritual being is at the center of who we are. Spiritual self-care is essential to our growth in relationship with God, bringing balance and sustenance to all areas of our life.

8. On a scale of 1 to 10, how would you evaluate your spiritual health?

1   2   3   4   5   6   7   8   9   10

Not healthy   Somewhat healthy   Very healthy

9. Spiritual health depends on spiritual nourishment. According to Matthew 4:4, where can we find that nourishment?

In Mark 12:29-30, Jesus quoted the original commandment given by God to the people of Israel in Deuteronomy 6:4-5. In the previous verses—Deuteronomy 6:1-3—God explained to His people that they could be healthy and prosperous if they would put Him first and obey the commandments He gave them. This passage speaks of how to be totally satisfied—with God and in every area of life. God promised them hope and a future; the fulfillment of that promise depended on the people's commitment and obedience to the Lord.

10. In practical terms what does it means to love the Lord your God with all your heart?

    With all your soul?

    With all your mind?

    With all your strength?

11. Paraphrase Mark 12:29-30, making it a prayer of commitment.

God wants us to love Him with our whole being because that is how He created us—as a whole person. We need to grasp the importance of emotionally, mentally, physically and spiritually good health.

12. Decide to which aspect of personal health each verse applies. Fill in the blank with the appropriate letter (*A* for body, *B* for soul, *C* for mind, *D* for spirit).

_____ " 'For my thoughts are not your thoughts' . . . declares the LORD" (Isaiah 55:8).

_____ "Man does not live on bread alone, but on every word that comes from the mouth of God" (Matthew 4:4).

_____ "Your beauty should not come from outward adornment" (1 Peter 3:3).

_____ "Do you not know that your body is a temple of the Holy Spirit?" (1 Corinthians 6:19).

_____ "An anxious heart weighs a man down, but a kind word cheers him up" (Proverbs 12:25).

_____ "How precious to me are your thoughts, O God!" (Psalm 139:17).

_____ "The lamp of the LORD searches the spirit of a man; it searches out his inmost being" (Proverbs 20:27).

_____ "May the words of my mouth and the meditation of my heart be pleasing in your sight" (Psalm 19:14).

ENDURING HOPE

The spirit of a woman either grows or is stunted based on how she thinks and feels about herself. If we are going to have a healthy body image, we need to change the way we think.

13. How do you view your body? Respond to each of the following statements (1 means strongly *disagree*, 5 means strongly *agree*).

	1	2	3	4	5
I feel pleased with the body I have.					
Maintaining a good spiritual life is a priority for me.					
I don't let my emotions control the way I think about myself.					
I like to think about what is good about me rather than what is wrong.					
Eating properly and exercising regularly are important to me.					
Spending time worshiping God satisfies something deep within me, and I do it often.					
I spend time each day reading and thinking about God's Word.					

Although balance is important, caring for our spiritual health must come first. "But seek first his kingdom and his righteousness, and all these things will be given to you as well" (Matthew 6:33). Studying God's Word, memorizing Scripture, praying and fasting are ways to grow spiritually, and they naturally help us become properly aligned in the other areas.

14. What area of your spiritual health do you need to ask God to help you with?

What first steps can you take to change?

As we've already discussed, when Jesus was asked which was the greatest commandment (see Mark 12:29-30), He quoted Deuteronomy 6:4-5. In verse 31, He added the second greatest commandment: "Love your neighbor as yourself."

15.   What does it mean to love your neighbor as yourself?

Loving ourselves is one of the hardest things for many of us to do. There are two things to remember: First, a healthy self-love is not prideful, but is based on who God is and His love for us (see John 3:16). Second, as we judge ourselves, so we judge others. Negative thinking produces negative thoughts, not only about us, but about others as well. As you consider these things, ask the Lord to help you change your attitude.

16.   According to Colossians 3:1-2, what should your attitude be?

When negative thoughts, emotions or attitudes creep in, we need to turn our focus toward Jesus.

EVERYDAY LIFE

Properly caring for your whole body is much more important to self-worth than how beautiful or intelligent you are. As you ask the Lord to help bring balance into your life by placing Him first, He will help you nurture the most important areas of who you are.

The Holy Spirit's role in your life is crucial to developing a healthy, holistic body image.

17. Summarize the following verses to show the Holy Spirit's role in a believer's life.

John 14:16-17

John 16:13

Romans 8:14-16

Galatians 5:22-23,25

18. What are the steps to living a holy life as presented in Romans 12:1-2?

Has the Lord shown you an area that He would like to renew? Ask Him to help you. Whenever you begin to feel critical about yourself in some way, stop and ask whether the thought or action is in-line with what God says about you. Who knows, you could lose five pounds without trying very hard! At the very least, you will accomplish God's purpose for you.

Note
1. This story is based on actual events and is used with permission.

*My son, do not forget my teaching, but keep my commands in your heart,
for they will prolong your life many years and bring you prosperity.*

PROVERBS 3:1-2

EVERYDAY WOMAN

Gail sat on the edge of the bed watching her granddaughter, Heather, play with her new baby. Gail smiled as she began to reflect on how fast the years had gone by. "I remember when you were that age, Heather. My, how precious you were. Now it's your turn to be the mom."

"Oh, Grandma," Heather sighed, "There are days when I just wonder what kind of mom I will be. Sometimes I get so nervous thinking about Jody's growing up."

Gail nodded knowingly. "I felt the same way. Just remember this: She will go through many stages. These first years will seem hard because she will be totally dependent on you, and you will question whether you are doing things the right way. Just remember that the most important thing is that she knows you love her and that you are there for her. Don't worry about making mistakes; they are inevitable, but your love and sincerity will make up for them. As she grows, you will think she doesn't really need you as much anymore, but truthfully, she will—just in different ways. Ah, Sweetie, you will do just fine."

Heather replied, "Sometimes I get scared because I know how much trouble I caused Mom and Dad at different times. I don't want Jody to make those same mistakes."

Gail chuckled, "Yes, but look at you now! What would life be without challenges?"

Again Gail reflected, this time thinking about her own life and the events that had marked each stage. Some stages had been much easier than others, but all of them have contributed to the person she is now. What would come next she wasn't sure; right now she was simply going to enjoy this moment with Heather and Jody.[1]

⚘

Each woman's life naturally progresses through various stages of development. These stages are not something to be feared but to be anticipated. As we take a more in-depth look at these stages, you will see how these stages have influenced the person you have become, as well as how God uses them to fashion you into the woman He created you to be.

1. How can understanding the stages of a woman's life help us understand and appreciate others?

The following are brief descriptions of the six stages of a woman's life. At each stage that you've been through, reflect on what it was like, including what you were like; what your relationships with your parents, family and peers were like; any major events (good or bad) that affected you; and whether it was a good, not-so-good or even traumatic stage of life. **Note:** These stages are based on generalities and ideal situations; none of us has experienced these stages as perfectly as they are listed here. They are meant as a guideline of how we develop as women during the normal life stages.

Stage One: 0 to 5 Years

This is a foundational stage of development, in which a baby is nurtured and loved for who she is. The parent is the primary caregiver and creates a safe environment for this precious gift. At age three, she begins to understand herself as a girl; she notices differences between men and women (i.e., makeup, shaving, clothing, etc.) and has a healthy regard for both. Day care, preschool and social events introduce her to other influences. Her primary caregivers are her role models at this time.

Stage Two: 6 to 9 Years

Her self-esteem is intact at this stage. She has a sense of hope and adventure, a desire to explore her world and to discover how she fits in it. She develops girlfriends, is close to her mother and likes to talk with her dad. It is an age of discovery. She begins to understand who God is and that sin separates her from Him.

Stage Three: 10 to 20 Years

This stage marks the onset of puberty. A girl becomes a woman and then a girl again, caught in that stage between childhood and adulthood. It is a time of hormonal development as her body takes the shape of a woman. Her world begins to change. She becomes more tempted by peer pressure, develops an interest in boys and tends to argue with her mother more frequently. Physical changes to her body affect the way she thinks about herself, resulting in emotional highs and lows. It is a very awkward time. As she reaches her late teens, she starts to develop a sense of identity apart from her mom and dad. What parents, teachers and others perceive as rebellion is actually an important part of this stage as she develops her own identity as a young woman.

Stage Four: 21 to 40 Years

The lifestyle choices a woman makes during this stage will shape the rest of her life. She understands her sexual identity and is comfortable with herself as a woman. Her body is at its peak physically and should function at its best. It is probably the busiest time of a woman's life. Decisions about career, marriage and family are generally made during this stage as she begins to recognize her gifts and influence. It can be a challenge for her not to neglect her body, mind, soul and spirit during this stage, as she can be under such pressure to take care of others. When she looks in the mirror, she sees the face of her mother more and more and begins to realize the tremendous influence her mother had on her.

Note: Many women become so busy during this stage of life that they neglect regular tests such as PAP smears and mammograms. These tests are extremely important and should not be overlooked. Check with your doctor to determine how frequently you should undergo such tests.

Stage Five: 41 to 60 Years

This is the time when the lifestyle choices she made earlier begin to play a big role. Women begin to go through menopause at this stage. Menopause is a crossroads in a woman's life; she realizes that her reproductive role is over and yearns to find a new one. Stressful events such as children leaving home—leaving no one to care for—often take place during this stage, adding to the emotional highs and lows. Hot flashes and mood swings are physical and emotional indicators of what she is going through. While proper nutrition, exercise and a healthy self-attitude toward aging are extremely important in this stage, it is also wise to have a good relationship with a trusted gynecologist who can evaluate her hormone levels. With proper physical care, this stage is a time for accomplishing goals she set aside years before.

Stage Six: 61+ Years

There are many factors that influence this stage of a woman's life. Her quality of health, retirement and the death of her spouse can sometimes overshadow her perception of aging by forcing her to make weighty decisions regarding her future. As she redefines her identity, she realizes she enjoys the freedom and flexibility that these years bring. Past menopause, she begins to understand herself as having a new purpose. There are greater opportunities at this stage to be active in her community, to enjoy grandchildren and to have mentoring relationships. She is not affected by the view of some that she is past her prime but instead seeks to make every day count.[2]

2. Of the stages you have already experienced, which has been the most enjoyable? Why?

Which has been the most difficult? Why?

There are many factors within these six stages that greatly impact our lives, including marital status: single, married, divorced or widowed. With the exception of marriage, the development of these life situations is unplanned. No one plans on her marriage ending in divorce; few would say they will remain single their entire life; widowhood is something that a married woman knows could happen but hopes never will. Each of us is in one of these stages.

3. Which of these four characterizes your life at this moment?

What are the positive aspects of your situation?

What has been hard?

How has God been with you?

No matter in what stage or circumstance of life we find ourselves, there is one constant in our lives—our Lord and Savior. He "is the same yesterday and today and forever" (Hebrews 13:8).

ETERNAL WISDOM

It's a fact: Life just doesn't stand still! We can lock ourselves in a house away from those ultraviolet rays of the sun. We can go to the best salons. We can search for the fountain of youth. No matter what we do, life slips by one second at a time. We can either appreciate each stage of development or we can moan and groan our way through life. How we go through the various stages of life can be one of the biggest factors in our self-perception and in the quality of life we live.

Everything that you have experienced in life has brought you to the point at which you are right now. Both good and bad situations have helped shape the season in which you find yourself now.

4.   How does Ecclesiastes 3:1-8 relate to understanding the stages of life?

Understanding the stages of our life not only helps us know ourselves, but it helps us have a more positive attitude toward others as well. Throughout the Bible, God gives us lessons on our worth at different stages of life—lessons on how to have a good quality of life, as well as how to respect others.

5.   The book of Proverbs provides wise counsel to help us through all stages of life. How does Proverbs 3:1-4 relate to living well through all stages of life?

6. How does Proverbs 3:21-24 relate to living well?

7. What are the benefits of a life with God, as described in the following verses?

Psalm 37:25

Psalm 92:12-15

Romans 8:16-17

The natural progression of a woman's life through the various stages is not something to be feared but to be anticipated. Each stage has its own joys and sorrows, challenges and triumphs. As you develop a clearer understanding of how these stages have influenced who you are today, you will be able to see how God uses each stage to help you become the woman He created you to be.

ENDURING HOPE

During the different stages of our life, we may encounter detours that get us off track—like forks in a river that flow away from the main course. These divergences have two possible effects: We can either let God use them to draw us closer to Him, or we can pull away and let them beat us up until we are far from God and living without purpose.

To illustrate this concept, let's draw a picture. You'll need a sheet of paper—at least 8½ by 11 inches. Read the following directions before getting started. Take your time with this project; allow the Lord to give you a fresh revelation about your life.

Part One

On your sheet of paper, draw a picture of a river that starts in the mountains and flows down to the ocean. You will need room to write later, so allow enough space. You may want to include:

- A creek that flows into the river from a spring, waterfall, etc.
- A creek that splinters off and then returns to the river downstream.
- A creek that moves away from the river and flows into the ocean at a different point.
- A creek that moves away from the river and then disappears, drying up.
- Waterfalls, rapids, ponds, lakes, etc.

Think about the life of this river. What happens to it along the way? What is its ultimate destination? Imagine that your drawing represents the life of a woman without God. She is born, she travels through life, and then she faces eternity without God. She hasn't necessarily rejected God; she just doesn't have a concept of who He is. Think of a neighbor or coworker. What is the ultimate destination of such a river?

Part Two

Now look at your drawing as a snapshot of your own life, from the perspective of a woman who has given her life to Jesus. Complete your picture with the following:

- Write your name, date and place of birth at the beginning of the river. Read Psalm 139:15 and Jeremiah 29:11; write those references at the beginning of the river.
- Draw lines across the river to signify the stages of development you have gone through to date. You may color code the stages or write them in if you wish.
- Mark the spot where you accepted Christ. Read John 7:38. If there is a verse that has been significant to you since you became a Christian, write it here.
- Read John 14:16-17, and then write the text in the flow of the river.
- Complete your picture by adding the major events in your life, as well as any verses that hold special meaning for you.

8. What has God shown you through this exercise?

EVERYDAY LIFE

So far we have seen that we must go through the stages of life, that life is futile without God, and that there are factors beyond our control that we have to deal with and ask God to bring healing to. We have also learned that, although we may have made some bad decisions along the way, God wants to forgive us and help us stay on the course He has planned for us. In Christ, we have acceptance and forgiveness from our loving God; and He desires that we enjoy life, each other and His presence.

9. Look at the river of life that you drew. Where along the river are you?

10. What is good about your life at this point?

11. What would you still like to see happen in your future?

What steps can you take to see that those things take place?

12. Do you have a Scripture that fills you with hope or gives you direction? Write it below and memorize it. If not, ask the Lord to give you one.

God wants us to live with purpose during each stage of our life. Be a woman with attitude—the attitude of Christ, that is (see Philippians 2:5-11)! Choose to live with purpose and happiness. Get out of that chair—there's work to be done!

Notes

1. This is a fictional account. Any resemblance to actual events or people, living or dead, is purely coincidental.
2. "Life Stages," *Health 24*. http://www.health24.co.za/Woman/Life_stages (accessed December, 2003); Dr. Deborah Newman, *A Woman's Search for Worth* (Wheaton, IL: Tyndale House Publishers, 2002), pp. 40-45.

Femininity

Charm is deceptive, and beauty is fleeting;
but a woman who fears the LORD is to be praised.

PROVERBS 31:30

EVERYDAY WOMAN

A group of women were having lunch. They were enjoying their time together and laughing about different women's issues. Suddenly, one of them, Jan, asked the others, "What is femininity?"

"What do you mean?" someone responded.

"Well, you know, what does it mean to be feminine?" Jan continued, "The subject came up with a coworker, and I just didn't know what to say. Does it mean I am soft and sweet and wear dresses all the time? I tried to think of a definition but just didn't know what to say. It's not something I usually think about, but now it's eating me, so I thought I'd ask all of you." Jan stood up, batted her eyelashes and moved her hips from side to side. "Am I being feminine?" she asked. The group chuckled.

"If that's being feminine, then count me out!" someone shouted.

"Feminine is the opposite of masculine," someone else suggested, "and therefore, gentle, more relational."

The ladies looked at one another with inquisitive looks and then began talking all at once.

"Does it have to mean feminism?"

"No, it's a certain quality; it's part of being a woman."

"How about sexy, alluring?"

After a few seconds of trying to decipher the hubbub, Jan spoke out, "Wait, wait, I can't hear everyone at once!" The ladies grew quiet. "That's good, now one at a time, tell me what you think, please. How can we define 'femininity'?"[1]

☙

There was a generation not many removed from ours that would have settled the question of femininity without much discussion. Then came the dawn of feminism. Some women (and men) felt liberated; others felt like they were losing their identity. Radical feminism has not only disrupted the social mores of our time, but it has also harmed women's understanding of themselves and twisted men's notions of their roles and attitude toward women.

As women's roles have changed over the last few decades, femininity has been greatly redefined. But when all is said and done, the heart of femininity is the essence of a woman: her characteristics, qualities and God-given design. The purpose of this session is to get to the core issue of femininity by identifying those things that have tainted our view of what being a woman is all about and then removing them to see what is really at the core of femininity. By realizing God's design, you will see how being female is a gift in all areas of your life, enabling you to be a better person, wife, mother, employee, leader and member of the Body of Christ. God wants you to enjoy your unique qualities and let them shine in whatever stage of life you are in.

1. Define "femininity" as you understand it.

2. List at least five traits that you think express femininity.

3. What influences from a woman's environment might affect the way she sees herself?

4. Give examples of comments that give a woman a negative image of femininity.

5. List five characteristics that people mistake for femininity.

Being female is part of our DNA. We should enjoy that fact! Some of the very things we are criticized for are qualities that should be allowed to grow and be expressed.

6. Think about three women you admire. Which qualities of theirs stand out to you?

7. What feminine qualities do you admire most about women? Why?

Whether in the workplace or in the home, femininity is in each of us simply because we are women. Our feminine characteristics allow us to be nurturing, caring, loving, emotional, relational, alluring and so on.

ETERNAL WISDOM

The ladies in our story had a difficult time coming up with a definition for "femininity." Perhaps they were afraid of giving a wrong answer, or maybe they thought the term "feminine" would label them as old-fashioned. Is femininity something to achieve or avoid? It may be helpful to think of femininity in terms of what distinguishes a woman from a man—her female qualities.

8. As you read Proverbs 31:10-31, note words or phrases that describe feminine qualities (you may wish to underline or circle them in your Bible).

    What nurturing qualities did this woman possess as a wife and mother?

9. What feminine qualities helped her excel in the marketplace?

10. What three feminine qualities are mentioned in verse 30? What does it say about them?

    How does that differ from the world's view of how these qualities should relate to femininity?

Although this passage is a bit intimidating to most of us, this woman is an excellent example of how to use feminine qualities to complement individual strengths for God's glory. Instead of feeling overwhelmed by impossibility, ask God to make this passage applicable to your specific situation.

11. From what you have learned about the woman in Proverbs 31, which qualities do you also possess?

Which qualities would you like to develop or improve?

The ladies in our story had a difficult time defining "femininity" because they were trying to reconcile it with modern society's philosophy that in order for a woman to prove herself, she has to act like a man; she has to let go of her softness, gentleness and cooperative nature to become a competitive, driven individual. However, as more and more women enter the workplace, businesses are beginning to realize that women possess unique abilities and intuitiveness that complement men. That shouldn't come as a surprise—it was God's plan from the very beginning!

12. Did the woman in Proverbs 31 use manly characteristics to accomplish her tasks? Explain.

What was her husband's attitude toward her role in the marketplace?

Before Eve was created "for Adam no suitable helper was found" (Genesis 2:20). Adam needed a helper—someone who had the qualities that he was missing, to complement him and help him get the job done. Eve was that missing piece. Together—as one—Adam and Eve represented the image of God (see Genesis 1:27).

13. Read Genesis 2:24. What does "become one flesh" mean? Does it mean that married men and women lose their identity as individuals?

14. How can a man and a woman help one another find their identity?

15. What feminine qualities can help build up the relationships between men and women, rather than tear them down?

ENDURING HOPE

The Bible is full of examples of women who used their God-given, feminine characteristics to accomplish their objectives. Some of them used them for good, others to promote their own agenda or to manipulate those around them. The Bible also gives women guidelines on how to use their femininity for His glory.

Read each Scripture passage below. Write the feminine quality portrayed and how it was (or could be) used. Then write whether it is a good or bad use of femininity.

Scripture	Quality	How Was It Used?	Good or Bad ?
Judges 16:15-20			
1 Samuel 25:2-35			
2 Samuel 20:15-22			
Esther 5:1-8; 7:3-4			
Proverbs 6:24-26			
Proverbs 11:16			
Proverbs 12:4			
Proverbs 21:9,19			
Acts 5:1-10			
Acts 9:36			
Acts 16:13-15			
1 Peter 3:1-2			
1 Peter 3:3-5			

16. In what ways have you neglected the positive feminine qualities you possess?

Up to this point we have focused on the attributes of femininity. Now let's discuss the physical side of being feminine.

17. In Song of Songs 7:1-9, what does the lover say about his bride?

18. According to Song of Songs 1:5-6, what does the beloved say about herself?

The lover describes her external beauty, but deep down he is drawn to her internal beauty. He does not even mention her dark skin, though she perceives it as a flaw. And so it is with us; we dwell on our external flaws and want to hide them in any way we can. We need to recognize that our femininity—our femaleness—is a gift from God to be used by and for Him.

19. Drawing from what you have learned in this lesson, what does being feminine mean to you?

20. What are a few ways you can exercise your femininity for God's glory and for the good of others?

What would God say to you about your femininity? Read the following acrostic. Create your own acrostic on the right, one that describes who you are as a woman.

W—Wisdom   W — _____

O—Overcomer   O — _____

M—Minister   M — _____

A—Amazing   A — _____

N—Noble   N — _____

Note

1. This is a fictional account. Any resemblance to actual events or people, living or dead, is purely coincidental.

Sexuality

Shout for joy to the LORD, all the earth. Worship the LORD with gladness;

come before him with joyful songs. Know that the LORD is God. It is he who made us,

and we are his; we are his people, the sheep of his pasture.

PSALM 100:1-3

❧

EVERYDAY WOMAN

At 32 years old, Sarah was living her worst nightmare. When her four-year marriage was cut short by divorce, her life shattered into tiny pieces. Coping with sudden singleness was a lot harder than she ever thought it could be. Not only had she lost her companion, but she had also lost her lover—the man who had held her close every night. She missed the nearness and intimacy they had shared in those early years. The sexual and emotional desires she had felt before marriage were now twice as strong. Now that she knew what it was like to have physical intimacy, deprivation ripped at her soul.

Sarah began to distance herself from her married friends. It was just too hard to listen to how wonderful their husbands were. Dating had no appeal; her heart was still wounded. But her yearning for someone to hold her grew daily. As a Christian, Sarah knew she was held to a high standard of sexual purity.

Needing an outlet, Sarah joined the singles group at her church. At first she was disappointed that the group consisted entirely of women; but as they discussed their desires and longings, Sarah realized she was not alone. These women had experienced similar feelings of guilt and longing. That camaraderie made each lonely night more bearable for Sarah. Their understanding and compassion helped her face—and overcome—her desires. While the physical longings still gnawed at her, she took great comfort in knowing that she wasn't the only one struggling with a loss of intimacy.

Although nothing could completely assuage her physical desires, they no longer consumed her thoughts and feelings. She began to feel better about herself as she relied on God's strength to help her through each difficult moment. Sarah began spending more time reading her Bible. Sometimes songs of praise would well up inside of her as she contemplated His goodness, power and love. One day she recognized that He was beginning to fill the empty places in her heart with His love. The difficult journey of rediscovering who she was as a woman wasn't over, but at least it had begun.[1]

Like Sarah, many women feel they have lost their sexual identity due to death or divorce. In such situations, the road to healing is often a long and lonely one. However, all women—whether single, married, divorced or widowed—are susceptible to believing that sexuality necessarily includes a satisfying sex life that defines who we are. One of women's most basic needs is to be loved and to be able to express that love to another. How she deals with this God-given need will define how she views her own sexuality.

1. How would you define "sexuality"?

Women often receive mixed messages concerning their sexuality from their families, the Church and the culture in which they live. When society puts God and moral principles on the shelf, an attitude of "do whatever feels good" runs rampant and physical satisfaction becomes the ultimate goal. The Christian woman is then faced with a dilemma: She wants to put God first in her life, but the temptation to conform to the world's standards is great.

2. Who or what in your life has had the greatest impact on defining your view of sexuality?

Many Christian women have difficulty even talking about the subject of sexuality. Broaching the subject with a woman (or group of women) you respect can help you feel more comfortable opening up. You will find that many women share your questions and struggles. It's also never too late for you to receive healthy sex education—for your own benefit, and for your children's benefit since it will enable you to pass along correct information to them.[2]

3. Why do women have difficulty being open and honest about the subject of sexuality? Explain.

4. What factors contribute to the way a girl thinks about herself sexually?

There is a difference between a healthy sexual attitude based on God's original design and a sexual attitude based on social and cultural values. Understanding the former is another step in our journey to discovering self-worth, as we learn to enjoy being women created in the image of God.

ETERNAL WISDOM

A woman—made in the image of God—is both physical and spiritual. The physical is really a manifestation of what is in the heart and soul of a woman. God's design for sexuality, then, must include both physical and spiritual elements.

5. What is the psalmist's attitude in Psalm 100?

6. What should your attitude be concerning God's design of you?

God designed physical intimacy to be more than a sexual act. For you as a woman, it involves a healthy ability to love a man deeply, to know him intimately as you search his heart and yield yours. In this process, you become more like Christ.

Ephesians 5:22-33 describes many ways that Christ is our example in marriage relationships. As you read the passage, complete the following chart:

	Christ's Example	Our Response
Ephesians 5:23-24		
Ephesians 5:25		
Ephesians 5:26		
Ephesians 5:27		
Ephesians 5:28		
Ephesians 5:29-30		
Ephesians 5:31-33		

In verse 32, Paul explained that he was talking about Christ and the Church. This passage applies to us on two levels. First, as female members of the Body of Christ, we can relate to the idea that the Church is the Bride of Christ. But we can also apply these verses quite literally to a marriage relationship.

The greatest act of love is to lay down one's life for another (see 1 John 3:16). True love involves desiring to come alongside a man to help him realize his full potential in every area of life. This is true intimacy. It is based on a secure, solid concept of sexuality, and it transcends the messages that society, culture, family and peers send us.

Sexuality in Marriage

Human sexuality finds completion in the intimate, sexual relationship of marriage. Both the physical and emotional aspects of sex give us an understanding of the oneness within the Godhead—complete connectedness and total abandonment to another in trust. The oneness of intimacy—the ecstasy of a sexual relationship between a man and a woman—completes God's design.

The marriage relationship is consummated in the act of sex. It is a gift from God to be enjoyed and treasured. Proverbs 5:15-19 is a picture of faithfulness within marriage.

7.   Summarize Proverbs 5:15-19 in your own words.

In Song of Songs 5:2-6 the bride was asleep when she heard her lover knocking. Before she could arise, he had already left. She longed for him and went looking for him in the middle of the night.

8.   Describe this woman's love for her husband.

The vows that a man and woman speak in the marriage ceremony allude to how a husband and wife grow in a marriage relationship. Words such as "know," "love," "honor," "respect" and "trust" must become part of their vocabulary and translate into action.

9.   How do knowledge, love, honor, respect and trust nurture a marriage into a strong and healthy relationship?

A strong, healthy marriage takes time to develop. Intimacy in marriage involves sacrifice, but when two people are committed to one another, the rewards far outweigh the complexities.

Sexuality in Singleness

If you are single, healthy sexuality starts with understanding that you are just as valuable as a married woman. You also have emotions, longings and physical desires that you want fulfilled, just as a married woman does. A healthy view of sexuality allows you to appreciate your femaleness, knowing that your value lies in who you are as an individual, not in whether you are single or married.

Let's use Sarah, our Everyday Woman, as an example.

10. Briefly describe Sarah's emotions, the root of her sense of rejection and her needs.

11. How did this trial strengthen her walk with God?

12. How can God fill the empty spaces left by the loss of a spouse—whether by death or divorce?

Internal peace and satisfaction won't come by simply overcoming your emotional and physical needs; they will only come by allowing God to fill the empty spaces. Physical touch is powerful and a very real need, but feeling the embrace of God is even more powerful—as Sarah discovered.

ENDURING HOPE

Why do we look for love in all the wrong places, when true fulfillment—following God's design—is right before our eyes? Sex is the most intimate physical act two people can experience. It is designed to bring a man and a woman closer on every level—physical, emotional, mental and even spiritual. Every time you give of yourself sexually outside of marriage, you exchange a piece of yourself for momentary satisfaction. Let's look at three distortions of God's perfect design.

Sexual Activity Outside the Bonds of Marriage

Any sexual activity outside the union God created between a man and a woman is not only a sin, but it is also emotionally, spiritually and even physically harmful. Although extramarital affairs, prostitution and premarital sex are common all over the world, these acts fail to fill the deeper need for pure intimacy. A momentary gratification, these acts break the bonds of trust or inhibit the development of trust, and they distort the guilt-free gift God desires for a husband and wife. The good news is—as with each of the distortions of God's design—that hope, healing and freedom from sin and shame are available through Jesus Christ. We'll discuss that process in the Everyday Life section.

Sexual Addiction

Don't let the term "sexual addiction" fool you—it is more prevalent among women than you might think. Reading romance novels, visiting chat rooms, engaging in masturbation and even viewing Internet pornography are activities women are engaging in more now than ever before, and each can lead to sexual addiction. Of the three distortions of God's design, sexual addiction is the easiest to hide from others; for that reason, accountability and/or a support group are musts for women struggling with sexual addiction.

Homosexuality

The Bible is clear that homosexuality is a distortion of God's design for intimacy and friendship; however, homosexuality is not worse than any other sin. Homosexuality may be a result of childhood injuries (i.e., verbal, physical, spiritual or sexual abuse; neglect; etc.) and therefore can be healed through the power of the Holy Spirit and the help of a reputable Christian counselor.

13. What admonitions against sexual immorality are found in 1 Corinthians 6:18-20?

If we consciously or unconsciously decide to put our focus and dependence on physical relationships rather than on God, we will search in vain to find fulfillment.

14. What hope does 1 Corinthians 10:13 offer the person who is struggling with sexual sin?

Because you are God's daughter, God will never turn His back on you, no matter how far you have strayed from His design for your life.

15. Read John 8:1-11. What crime was the woman in this passage accused of committing?

What was Jesus' response to the Pharisees' accusations?

Can you relate to how this woman must have felt? Why or why not?

16. Read Romans 12:1-2. What steps might help someone caught in sexual sin get back on track?

Dealing with those who are struggling with sexual sin is a delicate balance between grace and tough love. On one hand, 1 Corinthians 5:11 says, "You must not associate with anyone who calls himself a brother but is sexually immoral. . . . With such a man do not even eat." Yet the entire Bible is laced with words of forgiveness, acceptance and love.

17. Describe the balance between not tolerating sin and loving people in the state they are in—and not waiting for them to change.

God calls us to bring hope and healing. Meditate on Isaiah 61:1-3, thinking of ways you can "proclaim freedom" for those captive to sexual sin.

EVERYDAY LIFE

Jesus came to redeem what was lost in the Garden of Eden. He came to heal and restore each of us in every area of our life, including sexual dysfunction. The scars of shame, guilt and hurt from sexual abuse or past sexual mistakes may seem permanent, but *Jehovah Rapha*—the Lord who heals—can make you whole once again. He desires to restore your brokenness. Will you let Him? Will you commit to doing your part? If so, the following steps are an excellent place to begin.

Steps to Healing and Wholeness

- Open your heart and commit your life to God anew. Cover each step of the healing process with honest, vulnerable prayer. Remember, you can't shock God!
- Ask God to enable you to let go of your past hurts and to remove the stranglehold they have on your soul. Allow Him to free you from what was not in your control.
- Acknowledge any sexual sins you have committed and humbly ask God to forgive you.
- Surround yourself with sisters in Christ who can keep you accountable and who can support you through the healing process.
- Seek out a reputable Christian counselor who can help guide you through the sometimes overwhelming and painful process of true healing.

These steps to healing and wholeness are not limited to sexual issues. They will also help guide you through the process of recovering from any form of habitual sin or deeply rooted hurt.

18. What is keeping you from complete healing?

What practical steps can you take this week to begin the process?

Note: If you and/or your spouse are experiencing problems with issues of sexuality or sexual addiction, we advise you to seek professional help through a reputable Christian counselor. Your pastor may be able to guide you in finding the right person, or you can call Focus on the Family's counseling department (1-800-A-Family or 1-719-531-3400) for a free consultation by a licensed counselor[3] and a referral to a national counseling service network of over 2,000 licensed counselors throughout the United States.

Notes
1. This is a fictional account. Any resemblance to actual events or people, living or dead, is purely coincidental.
2. For additional information about sexuality issues, visit www.family.org and www.pureintimacy.org.
3. Counselors at Focus on the Family are licensed in the state of Colorado.

Friendship

*My command is this: Love each other as I have loved you. Greater love has no one than this,
that he lay down his life for his friends.*

JOHN 15:12-13

EVERYDAY WOMAN

Rachel was in the prime of her life when she learned she had breast cancer.
Only 25 years old, she felt the sickness was indescribably unfair. She often
wondered, *What could I have possibly done to deserve this? Why has God handed me
a death sentence before I've even begun to live life?* The doctors told her that she
was lucky they had discovered the cancer so early. A mastectomy would save
her life, but it would change her body forever.

Shirley was an older woman in Rachel's church. When she learned about
Rachel's condition, she sought out the younger woman. Shirley, now 59, had
also had a mastectomy—20 years earlier. At first, Rachel ignored the phone
calls from Shirley; she thought no one else could understand her pain, no
matter how similar her experience might be.

The day before the surgery, Rachel stayed home, crying in misery. The
phone rang repeatedly, but she never answered it. Shirley showed up at Rachel's
house that day. Rachel wouldn't open the door, but Shirley was not deterred.
She stood on Rachel's doorstep, praying that God would change the young
woman's heart. At nine o'clock that evening, Rachel finally opened the door.

Shirley said nothing as she took Rachel in her arms and gave her the comfort Rachel wished her own mother had been alive to give. They spent hours talking about Rachel's fears and concerns. Shirley spoke of her own pain, described the horror she had felt and shared that her greatest fear had been that her husband would no longer see her as a complete woman.

The next morning Shirley arrived early to take Rachel to the hospital and spent the whole day in the surgery waiting room. Hers was the first face Rachel saw when she awoke. Though readjusting to her new body was difficult, Rachel took great comfort in knowing that she wasn't alone.[1]

⌘

Relationships—women are designed for them. A woman without strong feminine support struggles more with feelings of loneliness and inadequacies than one who has friends to relate to. Even the strongest, most independent woman needs friends. She may not feel that she has time for them, but she needs them in order to understand herself better as a woman and simply for the sake of companionship.

As Rachel discovered, relationships are vital. They help us grow and provide a safe place where we can feel comfortable and accepted. Intimate friendships with other women provide accountability and enrich every area of our life. Because of our friendships, we can walk through life, reassured that there is someone close by.

1. Rachel, like many women, had a hard time asking for and accepting help. Why is it difficult to ask other women for assistance?

    If you have a need, on whom do you call?

Women are generally more nurturing, sensitive and intuitive than men. They are also generally more relational. Women have an innate need for friendships. Reflect on the stages of life we discussed in session 4. Within the first three years of a girl's life, she begins to understand her nature as a female and begins to form friendships. Relationships—especially female ones—play a big part in each of the subsequent life stages.

2. Who were your best friends in grade school? What were they like?

Did you stay close with these friends during high school, or did you develop new ones?

3. After high school, did your teenage friendships remain or grow apart? Was there a particular reason?

4. If you moved frequently during your childhood, it may have been difficult for you to nurture friendships. If this was the case, describe your childhood years and how you handled the relationships you did have.

5. As an adult, what do you value most in a friend?

Let's look at two biblical examples of strong friendships.

The following biblical examples represent the intimate friendship that is born from a strong understanding of God and self and from security in the relationship.

David and Jonathan

In 1 Samuel 18—20, we learn about the friendship between David and Jonathan. Their relationship began when King Saul (Jonathan's father) welcomed David into his household because of his bravery in fighting Goliath. But when Saul turned his heart away from God, he became depraved. As news of David's victories in battle spread, the people began to praise David and compared him to the king. This ignited jealousy in Saul's heart, and he vowed to kill David, even though he had at first loved him as a son. Despite his father's anger, Jonathan loved David as a brother and vowed to help him at all costs. As a result, Saul accused Jonathan of being a disgrace to his mother because he had chosen to befriend Saul's enemy rather than obey his father.

6. What characterized David and Jonathan's friendship, according to the following verses?

   1 Samuel 18:1-4

   1 Samuel 20:12-17,41-42

   2 Samuel 1:25-26

7. In describing his friendship with Jonathan, David said Jonathan's love was "more wonderful than that of women" (2 Samuel 1:26). What do you think David meant by this?

8. According to 1 John 3:16, how did David and Jonathan's friendship compare with the love Jesus Christ demonstrated for us?

9. Although David and Jonathan were men, their relationship can teach us much about the attributes of a solid friendship. List the qualities of a strong and lasting friendship.

Let's now look at a biblical example of a friendship between two women.

Ruth and Naomi

The book of Ruth is only four chapters long. It is highly recommended that you read the book in its entirety in order to fully grasp the remarkable friendship between this mother and daughter-in-law.

After the death of her husband and sons in the land of Moab, Naomi decided to return to her home in Judah.

10. In Ruth 1:8-13, what did Naomi urge her daughters-in-law to do?

11. What do verses 9, 10 and 14 tell us about the relationship between Naomi and her daughters-in-law?

12. What characteristics of a close friendship are found in Ruth 1:16-17?

13. If you read all four chapters, summarize Ruth and Naomi's attitudes toward each other and the relationship that developed between them.

It is possible that David and Jonathan were about the same age, while Ruth and Naomi were many years apart. It is good to have friends that are your own age, but it is also good to develop friendships with women of other ages. Titus 2:4-5 teaches that the older women are to teach the younger by their example. Conversely, the younger women can offer a youthful joy that we often lose as we grow older.

ENDURING HOPE

Strong friendships take work. Only weeds grow if we do not tend the garden! A beautiful friendship must be planted, watered, fed, weeded and nurtured. Let's look at the characteristics that make a friendship grow.

14. Match each characteristic of a strong friendship with the corresponding Scripture.

___ Rejoices and sorrows with you	a. Ruth 1:8
___ Loves at all times	b. Ruth 1:16-17
___ Encourages the other	c. Proverbs 16:28
___ More concerned for friend than self	d. Proverbs 17:17
___ Encourages spiritual growth	e. Proverbs 27:6
___ Is loyal	f. Ecclesiastes 4:9-12
___ Carries the other's burdens	g. Romans 12:15
___ Keeps confidence and doesn't gossip	h. Galatians 6:2
___ Gives correction in love	i. Philippians 1:8-11
___ Minimizes offenses	j. 1 Thessalonians 5:11
___ Strengthens and helps the other	k. 1 Peter 4:8

All of the preceding characteristics of friendship are epitomized in John 15:12-13: "My command is this: Love each other as I have loved you. Greater love has no one than this, that he lay down his life for his friends."

15. Who in your life have you felt God nudging you to get to know better? Ask Him to show you what the first step should be and to give you the courage to take it.

Friends enrich our life. They help us understand ourselves better, both what we are and what we are not. As iron sharpens iron, so our friends help us grow, mature and become more balanced, giving us a greater sense of self-worth (see Proverbs 27:17).

EVERYDAY LIFE

Sometimes friendships come in the form of a mentoring, or coaching, relationship. These friendships need not be time consuming, but they allow a woman to grow as she gleans wisdom from someone who has already been where she is now. As the learner grows and matures, she will eventually come alongside the one who is guiding her, and they will share a friendship on the same level. Mentoring relationships come in many forms.

16. Check the boxes next to the areas in which you would like to be mentored. Underline the areas in which you believe God could use you to mentor to others.

   ❑ You are a new Christian who wants to grow in the Lord.
   ❑ You have known the Lord for many years.
   ❑ You have just begun working outside the home.
   ❑ You are a career woman who has been on the job quite some time.
   ❑ You are a newlywed.
   ❑ You are a mother who has lost her child.
   ❑ You are a divorced woman who is scared and lonely.
   ❑ You are newly widowed.
   ❑ You are a mother of young children.
   ❑ Other _____

This is obviously not an exhaustive list, but it should get you thinking about the many ways you can nurture—and be nurtured—through caring friendships.

17. In what ways was Ruth and Naomi's friendship a mentoring relationship?

Oftentimes a mentor receives as much benefit as the one being mentored. In what ways did Ruth bless Naomi's life?

Many people will pass through your life as acquaintances and nothing more. You will meet others whom you will get to know a little more but to whom you can't quite bare your soul. We all need a friend with whom we can be transparent and vise versa. If you have one or more such friends, be thankful; nourish and strengthen those relationships. If you don't, ask God to give you one. God is faithful; He will meet your need for a true friend.

Note

1. This is a fictional account. Any resemblance to actual events or people, living or dead, is purely coincidental.

BECOMING THE
Woman
GOD CREATED

The LORD will fulfill his purpose for me;

your love, O LORD, endures forever.

PSALM 138:8

EVERYDAY WOMAN

Marie was 22 when she began teaching Sunday School. Although she had difficulty relating to the young children, she had a heart to help. As time passed, however, she grew increasingly dissatisfied with her weekly lessons and impatient with the children. It wasn't that she didn't care for the children; she just felt like something was missing. She decided to switch to helping in the nursery. She adored the infants, but before long she experienced the same sense that helping in the nursery wasn't quite what she was supposed to be doing.

One Sunday after church, Marie happened upon a teenager named Cara who was crying uncontrollably in the women's restroom. As Marie consoled her, she learned Cara was pregnant. Afraid to tell her parents, her friends and her boyfriend, the girl was contemplating suicide to escape disappointing everyone who mattered to her. Marie listened carefully to Cara, offered advice and expressed concern, being careful not to appear judgmental. Realizing that someone did care about her, no matter what her sins, Cara decided to confess her situation to her parents.

Marie had an epiphany. She went to the local crisis pregnancy center the next day to volunteer. After only a week of service, Marie knew without a doubt that she had finally found the place where God wanted her to serve.

Marie had a desire to grow in her walk with Christ and to teach others to do the same, so a few weeks later Marie decided to call Cara. Cara was very excited to hear her voice. She had been praying that God would send a godly woman who could help her grow in her faith.

As the weeks and months passed, Marie's sense of self-worth grew as she exercised her God-given gifts and passions. She finally understood how fulfilling it could be to serve God and others.[1]

$$\propto$$

Each of us is defined by the core value of our life. For someone who does not believe in God, her universe revolves around self. Those who don't know God turn to scholars, philosophers, scientists, bars, movies, books, talk shows or whatever else sounds good to define who they are and how they will respond to life. To them religion may seem like a crutch, and most don't want any part in it. For those of us who are Christians, like Marie, God is at the center—the core—of who and what we are. He is not merely our crutch; He is our breath of life. He created us for relationship with Him and for His pleasure.

1. What do the following Scriptures tell us about God's design?

    Genesis 1:31

    Psalm 139:13-14

    Romans 1:20

2. How have you experienced God's plan in your own life?

God planned our lives before we were born. He desires for us to know Him well so that we can know ourselves. As we build a relationship with Him, He will help us enjoy the wonderful moments of life and will walk with us through the difficult ones.

ETERNAL WISDOM

Underneath all the layers of expectations imposed by others and self, the core of your self-worth lies in your relationship with God. That has been His design from the beginning.

3. According to John 3:16-18, how much does God love you?

What is required in order to have a relationship with Him? Do you have a growing relationship with Him?

Jesus Christ paid the price for us to have free and open access to God. Without a personal relationship with Jesus Christ, we cannot have intimacy with God. We can know of God, we can even believe that God exists, but without Jesus we are still held captive under the Law. If you are unsure about your relationship with Jesus, speak to your group leader, a Christian friend or your pastor.

4. According to Galatians 4:3-7, what are our rights as children of God and how do we obtain those rights?

It is the indwelling presence of God through Jesus Christ and through the power of His Holy Spirit that fills our whole being and restores us to an abundant relationship with the God of all creation. To grow as a woman of God, you must bring your whole self—body, mind, soul and spirit—into alignment with God's will and purpose. As you surrender to the lordship of Jesus Christ, your motto becomes "Not my will be done, but yours, Lord."

5. What does it mean to surrender your will to the lordship of Christ?

We must surrender our whole being to His lordship. What are you holding back from Him?

The more you grow in your relationship with God, the easier it becomes to see yourself as He originally designed you: a work of art displayed for His glory.

6. What does Psalm 138:8 tell you about God's work in your life?

A maturing woman of God is able to set self aside to see other people's lives and circumstances from His perspective, serving others with their well-being in mind. As we saw earlier in the study, true growth must include our whole being; it includes loving God with our whole heart, mind, soul and spirit (see Deuteronomy 6:5).

7. List the characteristics of spiritual growth as described in Colossians 1:9-12.

8. According to Romans 12:1, what is the greatest act of service and worship you can perform?

9. What general exhortation about our gifts is found in Romans 12:4-8?

Do you know your spiritual gift(s)? How are you using it (them)?

Do you truly want to grow in Christ? Exercise the gifts and abilities He has given you to serve others. It is only in doing what He has planned that you will find true fulfillment.

ENDURING HOPE

God has given each of us tailor-made abilities. He is pleased when we discover and use them to honor Him. Marie, our Everyday Woman in this session, learned this valuable lesson as she tried to find the best place to serve.

10. An example of a mature, godly woman who understood her gifts is found in Judges 4:4-16. Who was she, and what was her calling?

What did she accomplish because of her obedience?

11. Think of a woman you know who is using her gifts to serve others. Describe her.

God's Word feeds us, prayer sustains us, worship draws us, and fellowship nurtures us. Every element is vital to our growth. "He who began a good work in you will carry it on to completion until the day of Christ Jesus" (Philippians 1:6).

EVERYDAY LIFE

Prayerfully, ask the Lord to examine your walk with Him and show you where you are growing and where you need to improve.

12. In what ways are you progressing in becoming more Christlike?

13. Without being overly critical, in what areas is your walk with God weak?

What step will you take today to strengthen at least one area of weakness?

14. How do the following verses encourage you and give you hope?

Ephesians 1:17-19

Ephesians 3:14-21

Philippians 3:12-14

As this study comes to a close, take a moment to reflect on how far you have come and what you have learned. Write a letter to God, expressing what you have learned and how you have seen your value to Him. Include areas of your life that are still works in progress. Remember the words of Paul—we have not yet arrived, but we press on toward the goal (see Philippians 3:12-14)! Use a separate sheet of paper or your journal if you need more space.

Dear God,

Note

1. This is a fictional account. Any resemblance to actual events or people, living or dead, is purely coincidental.

WOMEN OF _____
Worth

General Guidelines

1. Your role as a facilitator is to get women talking and discussing areas in their lives that are hindering them in their spiritual growth and personal identity.

2. Be mindful of the time. There are four sections in each study. Don't spend too much time on one section unless it is obvious that God is working in people's lives at a particular moment.

3. Emphasize that the group meeting is a time to encourage and share with one another. Stress the importance of confidentiality—what is shared stays within the group.

4. Fellowship time is very important in building small-group relation-ships. Providing beverages and light refreshments either before or after each session will encourage a time of informal fellowship.

5. Encourage journaling as it helps women apply what they are learning and stay focused during personal devotional time.

6. Most women lead very busy lives; respect group members by beginning and ending meetings on time.

7. Always begin and end the meetings with prayer. If your group is small, have the whole group pray together. If it is larger than 10 members, form groups of 2 to 4 to share and pray for one another.

    One suggestion is to assign prayer partners each week. Encourage each group member to complete a Prayer Request Form as she arrives. Members can select a prayer request before leaving the meeting and pray for that person during the week. Or two women can trade prayer requests and then pray for each other at the end of the meeting and throughout the week. Encourage them to call their prayer partner at least once during the week.

8. Another highly valuable activity is to encourage the women to memorize the key verse each week.

9. Be prepared. Pray for your preparation and for the group members during the week. Don't let one person dominate the discussion. Ask God to help you draw out the quiet ones without putting them on the spot.

10. Enlist the help of other group members to provide refreshments, to greet the women, to lead a discussion group or to call absentees to encourage them, etc. Whatever you can do to involve the women will help bring them back each week.

11. Spend time each meeting worshiping God. This can be done either at the beginning or the end of the meeting.

How to Use the Material

Suggestions for Group Study

There are many ways that this study can be used in a group situation. The most common way is a small-group Bible study format. However, it can also be used in a women's Sunday School class. However you choose to use it, here are some general guidelines to follow for group study:

- Keep the group small—8 to 12 participants is probably the maximum for effective ministry, relationship building and discussion. If you have a larger group, form smaller groups for the discussion time, selecting a facilitator for each group.
- Ask the women to commit to regular attendance for the eight weeks of the study. Regular attendance is a key to building relationships and trust in a group.
- Whatever is discussed in the group meetings is to be held in strictest confidence among group members only.

Suggestions for Mentoring Relationships

This study also lends itself for use in relationships in which one woman mentors another woman. Women in particular are admonished in Scripture to train other women (see Titus 2:3-5).

- A mentoring relationship could be arranged through a system set up by a church or women's ministry.
- A less formal way to start a mentoring relationship is for a younger woman or new believer to take the initiative and approach an older or more spiritually mature woman who exemplifies the Christlike life and ask to meet with her on a regular basis. Or the reverse might be a more mature woman who approaches a younger woman or new believer to begin a mentoring relationship.
- When asked to mentor, someone might shy away, thinking that she could never do that because her own walk with the Lord is less than perfect. But just as we are commanded to disciple new believers, we must learn to disciple others to strengthen their walk. The Lord has promised to be "with you always" (Matthew 28:20).
- When you agree to mentor another woman, be prepared to learn as much or more than the woman you will mentor. You will both be blessed by the mentoring relationship built on the relationship you have together in the Lord.

There are additional helps for mentoring relationships or leading small groups in *The Focus on the Family Women's Ministry Guide*.

SESSION ONE: DEFINING WORTH

Before Each Meeting

The following preparations should be made before each meeting:

1. Gather materials for making name tags (if women do not already know each other and/or if you do not already know everyone's name). Also gather extra pens or pencils and Bibles to loan to anyone who may need them.

2. Make photocopies of the Prayer Request Form (available in the *Focus on the Family Women's Ministry Guide*), or provide 3x5-inch index cards for recording requests.

3. Read through your own answers, and mark the questions that you especially want to have the group discuss.

In preparations specific to *this* meeting:

4. Collect photos of different women from magazines. Select pictures that show different aspects and stages of womanhood: at play, at work, fat, skinny, young, old, sad, happy, confident, insecure, etc. Also have glue or transparent tape, a roll of craft or butcher paper (or several sheets of poster board) and masking tape or tacks. Attach the roll of paper (or poster board) to the wall using masking tape or to a bulletin board using tacks. Place the pictures on a table near the entrance to the room.

Ice Breakers

1. As each woman enters, make sure she makes a name tag and picks up a Prayer Request Form. Invite the women to look through the pictures you have collected and to select several pictures.

2. Have each woman introduce herself by describing herself in 10 words or fewer, or have each woman share her answers to question 1.

3. **Option 1:** Have the women make a collage of the pictures they selected. Invite them to share how each picture represents how the world views women. The goal here is to see various ways in which the media identifies women and tells us what we should or should not look like. Another goal is to identify the women's inner hearts by looking at the expressions on their faces. Have them brainstorm how the media tries to define our worth as women.

4. **Option 2:** If there isn't time to collect photos, invite members to describe images of women that are represented in the media. What does the media say about women?

Discussion

1. **Everyday Woman**—Discuss questions 2 through 4. Share some or all of the following information: **Self-worth is our basis for being. It is our identity, our reality, the substance of who we are. Another term is**

"self-identity." For a non-Christian the center of identity is the self. For a Christian the center of identity is Christ. As Christians we understand that God created us as unique individuals with a chemical makeup that is uniquely ours. No one else is like us. Self-worth defines us as a person. It includes our personality, our gender and our physical distinctions. From the time we are conceived our self-worth begins to take shape. As a small child it is shaped by our parents, family and friends. As we grow, other influences—such as teachers, the media and our culture—begin to alter the person that God created. Understanding our value is a journey to reclaiming aspects of worth that have been lost or covered up. Understanding our self-worth helps us to realize our significance as children of God. It enables us to become more productive people as we grow in God's grace and in the gifts of the Spirit.

2. **Eternal Wisdom**—Recite Psalm 139:13-14 together. Encourage the women to memorize the key verse of each session. Discuss questions 5 through 7. Invite volunteers to share how Psalm 139 has helped them understand their value in God's eyes. How has it changed their perceptions of God's love and thoughts toward them?

   Encourage them that it is OK if they don't feel like God did a very good job designing them. Perhaps one day they will come to appreciate His workmanship in them.

   Invite members to share the words or phrases that they underlined or noted. Explain: **Focusing on keywords is an exercise to help formulate a description of how God knows us and of who He is. His love is so intimate. He is our protector. He will destroy our enemies. Most important, He will never leave us. That means in our darkest hours or our most despairing moments, He is there. It is important to grasp this concept because it is our foundation for growing in Christ.**

3. **Enduring Hope**—Question 9 is deeply personal and your group may not be ready to share about past hurts. You do not want this to be a time to air dirty laundry either. Instead, ask for a show of hands of anyone who had a bad experience during elementary school that affected their self-image. Invite one or two volunteers to share *briefly*. Discuss questions 10 and 11. The psalms listed are meant to bring peace and hope. Discuss what these verses teach us about God.

Explain: **We make a choice as to whether we believe what God's Word says about us. If we say we believe it, then we need to live our life accordingly. In which area of your life are you having a hard time believing God?** After a few have shared, reread Psalm 139:13-14 and invite group members to share how they can apply these verses when they are not feeling valued.

> **Note:** This section might dredge up painful memories for some of the women. If you sense this is the case, do not try to be the problem solver. You can pray with these women, but encourage them to talk to a Christian counselor or pastor.

4. **Everyday Life**—This is a time to let each woman share what the significance of this lesson was for her. Invite volunteers to share their paraphrase of Psalm 139.

   Encourage members to share an area in which they do not feel worthy—something that they recognize as an area God would like them to focus on for the next week. Have them add this area to their Prayer Request Form. Then have each woman trade her prayer request with another woman in the group. Encourage them to pray for their prayer partner during the week and even to call one another during the week to check in.

5. **Close in Prayer**—Have everyone recite together the praise Scriptures (see question 13). Close in prayer, asking the Lord to specifically bless each woman.

6. **Encourage Scripture Memory**—One very effective way to heal the heart is to memorize God's Word. Encourage the women to try to memorize the key verse each week or to select a verse from the lesson that was especially helpful to them. Provide an opportunity at each meeting for the women to recite the memory verse. The *Focus on the Family Women's Ministry Guide* contains additional information on encouraging Scripture memorization.

After the Meeting

1. **Evaluate**—Spend time evaluating the meeting's effectiveness (see *The Focus on the Family Women's Ministry Guide*, "Beginning a Bible Study Program" section).

2. **Encourage**—During the week, try to contact each woman (through phone calls, notes of encouragement, e-mails or instant messages) and welcome her to the study. Make yourself available to answer any questions or concerns the women may have and generally get to know them. If you have a large group, enlist the aid of a few group members to contact the others.

3. **Equip**—Complete the Bible study.

4. **Pray**—Prayerfully prepare for the next meeting, praying for each woman and your own preparation. Discuss with the Lord any apprehension, excitement or anything else that is on your mind regarding the Bible study material or the group members. If you feel inadequate or unprepared, ask for strength and insight. If you feel tired or burdened, ask for God's light yoke. Whatever it is you need, ask God for it. He will provide!

Further Reading

Newman, Deborah. *A Woman's Search for Worth*. Wheaton, IL: Tyndale House Publishers, 2002.

Tompkins, Iverna. *The Worth of a Woman*. Plainfield, NJ: Logos International, 1980.

SESSION TWO: WHO AM I?

Note: This lesson is only an introduction to temperaments and is by no means exhaustive. There are many personality paradigms, and the purpose of using this fourfold model is simply to help women understand the basic strengths and weaknesses of each type of personality.

Before the Meeting

1. Make the usual preparations as listed on pages 83 and 84.
2. Prepare slips of paper for ice-breaker option 1.

Ice Breakers

1. **Option 1**—Give each woman a piece of paper listing questions about favorite color, activities, person, and whether they come alive in a group of people (extroverts) or prefer time alone (introverts). Instruct the women to answer with the first response that comes to mind. Invite each woman to share at least one favorite, thus encouraging everyone to share, even the quiet ones who might not usually talk.

2. **Option 2**—Invite volunteers to name someone who has their favorite personality. It could be an actor or actress, author, painter, musician, politician, news broadcaster, etc. Ask why they admire that personality.

3. Invite a volunteer to recite the memory verse from session 1.

Discussion

1. **Everyday Woman**—Go over the four personality types discussed in the session and ask the ladies whether they agree or disagree with the descriptions. Discuss the answers to question 5 (Jane: **Sanguine**; Sarah: **Phlegmatic**, Christy: **Choleric**, Monica: **Melancholic**).

2. **Eternal Wisdom**—Discuss the answers to questions 10 through 12.

3. **Enduring Hope**—Share the following strengths of each personality type:
   - **Sanguine**—enthusiastic, youthful, helpful
   - **Choleric**—natural leader, visionary, quick to respond in emergencies
   - **Melancholic**—passionate, creative, compassionate, thorough, organized
   - **Phlegmatic**—peacemaker, balanced, calm in the storm

   Share the following weaknesses of each personality type:
   - **Sanguine**—childish, not a good listener, disorganized
   - **Choleric**—prideful, too serious, pressures others to conform
   - **Melancholic**—needs to cheer up, perfectionist, often negative
   - **Phlegmatic**—procrastinates, too secretive, dislikes change

   Invite volunteers to share their key personality traits. Celebrate how the different personalities of the group members add richness to the group.

4. **Everyday Life**—Briefly explain how we can appreciate our personalities by looking at ourselves as God's workmanship. Then invite women to share what they wrote or drew as their masterpiece.

5. **Close in Prayer**—Form groups of two or three women to pray for one another. Have the women trade Prayer Request Forms, and encourage them to continue to pray for one another throughout the week.

After the Meeting

1. **Evaluate.**
2. **Encourage**—Instruct prayer partners to contact each other at least once in the coming week for encouragement and support. As the leader, try to contact each woman during the week. If the group is large, enlist the help of other women in the group—each volunteer can contact a smaller group of women.
3. **Equip**—Complete the Bible study yourself.
4. **Pray**—Prayerfully prepare for the next meeting, praying for each woman and for your own preparation.

Further Reading

Kroeger, Otto, and Janet Thuesen. *Type Talk*. New York: Delacorte Press, 1988.

Littauer, Florence. *Personality Plus*. Tarrytown, NY: F. H. Revell, 1992.

SESSION THREE: IT'S MY BODY

Before the Meeting

1. Make the usual preparations as listed on pages 83 and 84.
2. Make necessary preparations for the ice-breaker option you choose.

Ice Breakers

1. **Option 1**—Watch the last 10 to 15 minutes of the movie *Shrek* (about 1 hour and 20 minutes into the video). The scene begins with the marriage ceremony of Lord Farquaad and Princess Fiona, and continues until Shrek tells Fiona that she *is* beautiful despite her being an ogre.

Briefly discuss how Fiona viewed herself and the differences between what Lord Farquaad saw in Fiona and what Shrek saw in her.

2. **Option 2**—Have each woman draw a picture of her body or a picture of an animal that she feels represents her body. Discuss why she thinks this way. Let the group comment on one another's drawings.

3. Invite a volunteer to recite the memory verse from session 2.

Discussion

1. **Everyday Woman**—Briefly review the four aspects of health: physical, emotional, mental and spiritual. Invite volunteers to share their answers to questions 5, 7 and 9. Discuss what would happen if you took God out of the picture. Based on their current lifestyle, ask the women to project a humorous image of themselves in 10, 20 or 30 years.

2. **Eternal Wisdom**—Invite four volunteers to share one of their answers to the four parts of question 10. Briefly discuss the answers to question 12: **C, D, A, A, B, C, D, B**. They may have different answers; allow them to discuss their reasons.

3. **Enduring Hope**—Invite volunteers to discuss any part of question 13 that might have opened their eyes. Advise them that if they really want to change in a particular area, it's best to commit to one thing at a time. Discuss question 14; then read Proverbs 25:27-28. Discuss how this passage could be applied to changing their lifestyles to become healthier individuals.

4. **Everyday Life**—Discuss the role the Holy Spirit plays in a believer's life (from question 17). Explain: **Growth involves two elements: the Holy Spirit's empowerment and our action. Although God is capable of anything, He requires us to do our part.** Discuss: **Which is harder: trusting the Lord to enable you to do something or stepping out in faith to get it done?**

5. **Close in Prayer**—As a group, read Psalm 133; then, in pairs, have women pronounce a blessing on each other to bring fresh life, hope and faith into every area of their lives. Have these pairs exchange Prayer Request Forms.

After the Meeting

1. **Evaluate.**
2. **Encourage**—Encourage prayer partners to pray throughout the week for their partner's attitude about her body image, especially if she made a commitment for the week. Remind them that praying for someone else will also help them succeed!
3. **Equip.**
4. **Pray.**

Further Reading

Newman, Deborah. *Loving Your Body.* Wheaton, IL: Tyndale House, 2002.

Lewis, Carole. *First Place.* Ventura, CA: Regal Books, 2001.

SESSION FOUR: LIFE STAGES

Before the Meeting

1. Make the usual preparations as listed on pages 83 and 84.
2. If you plan to do the Enduring Hope activity option, you will need butcher paper or poster board, tacks or masking tape, and felt-tip pens.

Ice Breakers

1. **Option 1**—Go around the room and ask each woman to complete the phrase: "When I grow up, I want to be . . ."
2. **Option 2**—Ask each woman to share what her favorite stage of life has been and why, or invite group members to share their answers to question 2.
3. Invite a volunteer to recite the memory verse from session 3.

Discussion

1. **Everyday Woman**—Briefly review the various life stages. Invite group members to share their answers to question 1.

2. **Eternal Wisdom**—Discuss the question regarding Ecclesiastes 3:1-8. If you have a mixed-age group, ask the younger women to share one area in which they would like older women to understand their age group better. Ask the older women to give one area they wish the younger generation would understand about them.

   Form groups of three to four to discuss question 7 and the benefits and blessings of knowing God at a young age. Life is full of trials, unexpected events and unwanted detours. Have someone in each group read James 1:2-4, and then have them discuss God's perspective regarding trials in our lives.

3. **Enduring Hope**—Explain: **Sometimes we forget that Jesus had a human body and faced similar issues as He grew up.** With the whole group, discuss Jesus' life: His birth, temptations, struggles and successes.

   Discuss with the whole group what they saw about their lives when they looked at the finished map of the river they drew. Ask: **Is there anyone whose river is flowing backward? If so, read Philippians 3:13-14. If it isn't flowing backward, then it is flowing forward, which means that everything you are experiencing in life adds to the forward movement of your life. It may not seem like it at the time, but where there is motion, there is progress toward a final destination.** Explain how God's instruction and discipline are means to get a stagnated section of the river moving again.

   Activity Option—As a group make a map of Jesus' life similar to the ones the women drew of their lives. Discuss: **Was the journey down Jesus' river straight, or was it windy with side streams?** Discuss the result of Jesus' completing His journey, and His attitudes along the way.

4. **Everyday Life**—Ask: **Is your life out of control? In what ways?** After a few minutes of discussion, clarify: **We are either leading our life or letting it lead us. When it leads us, we are blown about in every direction. When we are doing the leading, we make the decisions that will determine the quality of life we lead, even when something happens that isn't in our realm of control.** Discuss how acceptance and forgiveness can affect their lives.

5. **Close in Prayer**—Allow a time for the group to pray for each woman who requests it. Close with a time of worship, giving thanks for God's perfect plan for each of our lives. Have women select a Prayer Request Form before they leave.

After the Meeting

1. **Evaluate.**
2. **Encourage.**
3. **Equip.**
4. **Pray.**

Further Reading

Newman, Deborah. *A Woman's Search for Worth*. Wheaton, IL: Tyndale House Publishers, 2002.

Partow, Donna. *A Woman's Guide to Personality Types*. Minneapolis, MN: Bethany House, 2002.

SESSION FIVE: FEMININITY

Before the Meeting

1. Make the usual preparations as listed on pages 83 and 84.
2. Prepare the necessary materials for the ice-breaker activity you choose.

Ice Breakers

1. **Option 1**—Serve cookies and tea on china plates and with teacups rather than using paper cups and plates. Ask: **Do you feel more feminine using fine china and dainty things? Why or why not?**
2. **Option 2**—Ask women to briefly share their views on feminism, both the pros and cons of the movement. Discuss: **Should feminism have a place in the Church and why?**
3. If you will be doing the activity option for Eternal Wisdom, prepare a handout (or write the following list on a poster board or white board and have paper available). Instruct members to write a résumé for themselves with the following information: name, household responsibilities, family responsibilities, family members they care for, educational experience, brief job description, any other pertinent information. They will use this sheet later.

4. Invite a volunteer to recite the memory verse from session 4.

Discussion

1. **Everyday Woman**—Invite volunteers to share their answers to questions 1 and 2. Discuss: **Is femininity something they feel comfortable with, are afraid of, or have a negative connotation of? What do they like the most about being a woman? In what ways (positive and negative) do women use their femininity to accomplish what they want?**

2. **Eternal Wisdom**—Discuss questions 8 through 12.

    Activity Option—Discuss questions 8 through 10 only. Then instruct group members to compare the résumé they wrote for themselves with the woman in Proverbs 31, noting their similarities and differences. Depending on age, life stage and responsibilities, most women are living a life similar to that of the woman in Proverbs 31.

    Discuss: **How can feminine characteristics help each woman be a better parent, wife, leader and coworker?**

3. **Enduring Hope**—Discuss ways in which we can take full advantage of our womanhood, such as exhibiting the fruit of the Spirit (see Galatians 5:22-23), dressing up for a special event, or pampering ourselves (e.g., getting our nails done or enjoying a hot bath). Be sensitive to women who have struggled with the issue of being feminine and have tried to hide their femininity by dressing and acting more masculine. Also look at ways in which women use their femaleness in a negative way (i.e., inappropriate dress, overly flirtatious behavior, pouting, etc.). Discuss Ephesians 5:1-2. **As women, how can we become imitators of Christ?**

4. **Everyday Life**—Discuss outward characteristics and appearance versus inner qualities and beauty. Invite volunteers to share what they learned about themselves from this lesson.

5. **Close in Prayer**—Ask the women to share their prayer requests with the whole group. Lead the group in a prayer of thanksgiving, glorifying God for designing women the way He did.

After the Meeting

1. **Evaluate.**
2. **Encourage.**
3. **Equip.**
4. **Pray.**

Further Reading

Van Leeuwen, Mary Stewart. *Gender and Grace.* Downers Grove, IL: Inter-Varsity Press, 1990.

SESSION SIX: SEXUALITY

Before the Meeting

1. Make the usual preparations as listed on pages 83 and 84.
2. Prepare the necessary materials for the ice-breaker activity.

Ice Breakers

1. **Option 1**—Divide the group into two teams. Give each team a poster board and a felt-tip pen. Give them two minutes to write down as many adjectives as they can think of that connote sexiness. Share the lists.
2. **Option 2**—Beforehand, collect magazine advertisements that show the many ways that sex is used to sell products. Display these on a bulletin board or poster board, or simply have women describe the ads they have seen that use sex to sell.
3. Invite a volunteer to recite the memory verse from session 5.

Discussion

1. **Everyday Woman**—Discuss questions 1 through 4. Explain: **Our concept of sexuality manifests itself in the way we talk, dress, move, behave and express ourselves.**

> **Note:** If your group consists of all married or all single women, focus on the issues pertaining to them; otherwise, don't let one group dominate the discussion.

2. **Eternal Wisdom**—Discuss questions 5 through 12 as appropriate for your group. Have volunteers share ways in which they are thankful they were created women.

3. **Enduring Hope**—Discuss how humanity has distorted God's design for human sexuality, as well as the meanings of love, acceptance and forgiveness. After discussing the question, ask: **How can we love and accept a person caught in sexual sin without condoning his or her lifestyle?**

4. **Everyday Life**—Explain: **Physical appearance is one aspect of our sexuality.** Brainstorm ways we can care for ourselves to enhance our appearance and have a better self-image (i.e., getting a different hairstyle, grooming nails, wearing clothes that fit nicely, wearing colors that complement skin tone, etc.). Explain: **The core issue is being a good steward of the body God has given you. Many women in Christian circles find it difficult to talk about sexuality.** Encourage a few volunteers to share how God has helped them see themselves as healthy, sexual women.

5. **Close in Prayer**—Close with a time of worship and end with prayer for those who would like it. If you have a large group, form groups of two or three women to pray for one another. Have women pick a Prayer Request Form before they leave.

After the Meeting

1. **Evaluate.**
2. **Encourage.**
3. **Equip.**
4. **Pray.**

Further Reading

Balswick, Judith, and Jack Balswick. *Authentic Human Sexuality*. Downers Grove, IL: InterVarsity Press, 1999.

Barton, Ruth Haley. *Equal to the Task*. Downers Grove, IL: InterVarsity Press, 1998.

SESSION SEVEN: FRIENDSHIP

Before the Meeting

1. Make the usual preparations as listed on pages 83 and 84.
2. Prepare the necessary materials for the ice-breaker activities you choose.

Ice Breakers

1. **Option 1**—The purpose of this exercise is to draw the women a step closer to one another. Prepare a handout with the following questions. Allow each woman to briefly share her answers. If you have an especially large group, form smaller groups to share answers.
   - What is your favorite color?
   - Do you have a pet? What is it? How did you decide on its name?
   - What annoys you the most?
   - What is your favorite time of day? Why?
   - Describe your favorite book.
   - What have you liked most about this Bible study?
2. **Option 2**—Describe the following scenario: **A gala event is being planned to honor those who have made a difference in people's lives. You have been invited and are asked to bring a special guest to honor.** Discuss: **Who would you pick and why?**
3. Invite a volunteer to recite the memory verse from session 6.

Discussion

1. **Everyday Woman**—Discuss questions 1 and 5. Although it was not a topic in this session, discuss how females of all ages can be cruel in

relationships. Ask if anyone would like to share a childhood memory of an example of cruelty. Why does this take place?

2. **Eternal Wisdom**—Discuss questions 7 through 9. Explain: **God's desire for any deep friendship is total abandonment and surrender—the attitude of laying your life down for another.** Discuss questions 10 and 11; then ask: **What kind of woman must Naomi have been before the death of her husband that her daughters-in-law would love her so?** Discuss questions 12 and 13 and Ruth's loyalty. **What did Ruth learn about God from Naomi?** Compare the relationship between Naomi and Ruth with most relationships today between a mother-in-law and a daughter-in-law.

3. **Enduring Hope**—Compare answers to question 14: **g, d, j, a, i, b, h, c, e, k, f.** Read John 15:12-13, and then discuss practical ways we can show a friend that we care for her: make a phone call, send a note, eat together, walk together, show empathy, pray together, etc.

   Discuss unhealthy friendships: **Are there times when you depend on someone else for your emotional needs rather than turning to the Lord? Do you struggle with putting female friendships above your relationship with your husband?** Discuss how they could change unhealthy friendships into healthy ones.

4. **Everyday Life**—Discuss mentoring relationships. Invite volunteers to share their mentoring experiences. Discuss ways they believe the Lord has nudged them to reach out to someone or to ask someone for help. **Did they do it? What was the result?**

5. **Closing Prayer**—There will likely be at least one woman in the group who struggles with friendships because of past hurts or present circumstances. Pray that God will lead all the women into healthy and vibrant friendships. Pray that each one will keep her eyes on Jesus in her relationships. Have women take the Prayer Request Form of someone for whom they have not prayed.

After the Meeting

1. **Evaluate.**
2. **Encourage.**
3. **Equip.**
4. **Pray.**

Further Reading

Brestin, Dee. *The Friendships of Women*. Wheaton, IL: Victor Books, 1988.

Stanley, Paul, and J. Robert Clinton. *Connecting*. Colorado Springs, CO: NavPress, 1992.

SESSION EIGHT: BECOMING THE WOMAN GOD CREATED

Before the Meeting

1. Make the usual preparations as listed on pages 83 and 84.
2. Prepare the necessary materials for the ice-breaker activities you choose.
3. Make photocopies of the Study Review Form (see *The Focus on the Family Women's Ministry Guide*, "Beginning a Bible Study Program" section).

Ice Breakers

1. **Option 1**—This should be a day of victory, and a day for sharing God's goodness. Ask the women ahead of time to volunteer to bring a special treat. Use nice dishes to make this a special day. Or even plan a nice breakfast, lunch or dinner to conclude this study.
2. **Option 2**—Ask if anyone pursued a new friendship or worked on rebuilding an old one as a result of last week's session. Then have group members share which lesson was the most difficult for them and why.
3. Invite a volunteer to recite the memory verse from session 7.

Discussion

1. **Everyday Woman**—Discuss questions 1 and 2. Ask: **What is one thing you would like to pursue in knowing God more intimately?**
2. **Eternal Wisdom**—Discuss the truth: **Underneath all the layers of expectations imposed by others and self, the core of self-worth lies in our relationship with God.** Discuss questions in this section that

are of particular importance to your group members. Question 3 provides an opportunity to invite members to commit their lives to Christ.

3. **Enduring Hope**—Ask: **How does discovering a healthy self-worth relate to helping others?** If there is time, discuss the different gifts that God gives us, using Romans 12:4-8 as a guide. Read Hebrews 4:14-16 and discuss the importance of approaching the throne of grace with confidence. Your church might have a spiritual gifts survey that you could offer to the women who would like to know what their gifts might be.

4. **Everyday Life**—This section is the culmination of what we have learned during the past eight weeks and charts the path these women will take from here. Have volunteers read the verses in question 14 aloud. Discuss: **What is the essence of these verses? How is that significant to believers?**

   Encourage volunteers to share a portion of the letter they wrote to God. Invite them to share a significant lesson they have learned from this study. Discuss: **How have you changed? How has your perception of yourselves changed?** Even if this study simply confirmed an already strong sense of value, have them share that too.

5. **Close in Prayer**—Have the women stand and hold hands. Read Ephesians 3:14-21 as a prayer for each woman. While still holding hands, have each woman speak a blessing out loud for the person on her left. If your group is large, break into two groups. Close with a time of worship.

After the Meeting

1. **Evaluate**—Distribute the Study Review Forms for members to take home with them. Share about the importance of feedback, and ask members to take the time this week to write their review of the group meetings and then to return them to you.

2. **Encourage**—Contact each woman during the week to invite her to the next Focus on the Family Women's Series Bible study.

Further Reading

Wagner, C. Peter. *Discover Your Spiritual Gifts*. Ventura CA: Regal Books, 2002.
Your Bible

New from Focus on the Family®
The Women's Ministry That Has It All!

Kit includes

- *The Focus on the Family Women's Ministry Guide*
- *Crafts and Activities for Women's Ministry*
- *Women of Worth* Bible Study
- *Healing the Heart* Bible Study
- *Balanced Living* Bible Study
- *The Blessings of Friendships* Bible Study

Focus on the Family Women's Series Kit
Group Starter Kit • Bible Study
ISBN 08307.33574
Available September 2004

Research shows that women are the backbone of Christian congregations in America,* but many are overwhelmed and in need of a break to reconnect with the Lord. Focus on the Family has **combined the best features of women's ministries**— Bible studies, prayer, fellowship, Scripture memory and activities—and created **new resources for women of all ages** so that they can *relax* and *reflect* on God.

By learning to define themselves based on God's Word, women will decrease their feelings of being inadequate and overwhelmed, and increase their sense of self-worth while joining in fellowship with God and other Christian women. Help women come together with **the new ministry that has it all!**

The Focus on the Family Women's Series
is available where Christian books are sold.

Gospel Light

*From Barna Research, *Women Are the Backbone of the Christian Congregations in America*, March 6, 2000.

We've Combined the Best of Women's Ministry for One Comprehensive Experience!

These resources provide a multitude of ideas for giving women the much-desired opportunity to get together and share different life experiences— joys and sorrows—to build deep, Christ-centered relationships.

Women of Worth Bible Study

Women often define themselves by what others expect of them. Many feel they come up short when they try to have it all—beauty, family, career, success. This study helps women find their true identity and purpose through their relationship with Christ. Includes topics such as defining worth, body image, femininity, sexuality and relationships.
ISBN 08307.33361

Healing the Heart Bible Study

This study helps women experience emotional and spiritual healing by understanding the hurts and pain in their lives and finding restoration through Christ. Topics include recognizing the effects of sin, mending your thoughts, forgiveness and letting go of the past.
ISBN 08307.33620

Balanced Living Bible Study

When women strive to do it all, they end up feeling stressed out, fatigued and disconnected from God. This study gives women the tools to balance the various demands on their time while maintaining an intimate relationship with God. Topics include why women overextend themselves, separating the important from the urgent and managing the pressures of life.
ISBN 08307.33639

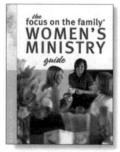

The Blessings of Friendships Bible Study

In today's fast-paced, busy world it's difficult for women to establish and maintain strong, healthy relationships. In this study, women will explore the nature of relationships and Christ's model for them. Some of the topics covered include forgiveness, being honest and vulnerable, the fine art of listening, receiving correction and the blessings of community.
ISBN 08307.33647

The Focus on the Family Women's Ministry Guide

This comprehensive guide gives leaders everything they need to set up and run an effective ministry for women of all ages and life situations.
ISBN 08307.33388

Crafts and Activities for Women's Ministry

This book is packed with ideas for adding fun and creativity to women's ministry meetings and special events. Includes reproducible craft patterns, activities and more!
ISBN 08307.33671

The Focus on the Family Women's Series is available where Christian books are sold.

Gospel Light

www.family.org   www.gospellight.com

STRENGTHEN MARRIAGES.
STRENGTHEN YOUR CHURCH.

Here's Everything You Need for a Dynamic Marriage Ministry!

Group Starter Kit includes

- Nine Bible Studies: *The Masterpiece Marriage, The Passionate Marriage, The Fighting Marriage, The Model Marriage, The Surprising Marriage, The Giving Marriage, The Covenant Marriage, The Abundant Marriage* and *The Blended Marriage*
- *The Focus on the Family Marriage Ministry Guide*
- *An Introduction to the Focus on the Family Marriage Series* video

Focus on the Family®
Marriage Series
Group Starter Kit
Kit Box
Bible Study/Marriage
ISBN 08307.32365

The overall health of your church is directly linked to the health of its marriages. And in light of today's volatile pressures and changing lifestyles, your commitment to nurture and strengthen marriages needs tangible, practical help. Now **Focus on the Family— the acknowledged leader in Christian marriage and family resources**—gives churches a comprehensive group study series dedicated to enriching marriages. Strengthen marriages and strengthen your church with **The Focus on the Family Marriage Series.**

The Focus on the Family Women's Series
is available where Christian books are sold.

Gospel Light